Published for
**OXFORD INTERNATIONAL
AQA EXAMINATIONS**

International GCSE
ENGLISH AS A SECOND LANGUAGE
Revision Guide

Dean Roberts

Li Ning

Heba Fathi Ghobrial

OXFORD
UNIVERSITY PRESS

Great Clarendon Street, Oxford, OX2 6DP, United Kingdom

Oxford University Press is a department of the University of Oxford.
It furthers the University's objective of excellence in research,
scholarship, and education by publishing worldwide. Oxford is a
registered trade mark of Oxford University Press in the UK and in
certain other countries

British Library Cataloguing in Publication Data
Data available

978-1-38-203385-5

10 9 8 7 6 5 4 3 2 1

Paper used in the production of this book is a natural, recyclable
product made from wood grown in sustainable forests.

The manufacturing process conforms to the environmental
regulations of the country of origin.

Printed in Bell & Bain (UK)

Acknowledgements
The publisher and authors would like to thank the following for
permission to use photographs and other copyright material:

Cover image: Jeffrey Coolidge/Getty Images

Photos: p92: imtmphoto/Shutterstock; **p94 (t):** Image Source / Alamy
Stock Photo; **p94 (b):** AFPhoto / Alamy Stock Photo;
p103: T photography/Shutterstock; **p173:** Dan Grytsku / Alamy Stock
Photo; **p175:** Kusalodom/Shutterstock.

Artwork by Andrew Groves and Oxford University Press.

Michael Clerizo: An extract of 517 words from the chapter '**Airport
tourism**' from the book: '***The Lonely Planet Guide to Experimental
Travel***' edited by Rachael Antony and Joel Henry (Lonely Planet, 2005).
Used with permission from the author.

AQA material is reproduced by permission of AQA.

Every effort has been made to contact copyright holders of material
reproduced in this book. Any omissions will be rectified in subsequent
printings if notice is given to the publisher.

Contents

Audio

All of the **audio** tracks are on the website at
www.oxfordsecondary.com/oxfordaqa-revision

How to use this book

This book uses a **Knowledge**, **Recap**, and **Apply** approach to your revision. It is important that you follow these in order as they work together to make your revision effective.

In the four main practice units, our focus is to help you prepare for assessment by offering you a lot of practice. In these units we provide guidance, tips, input from examiners, and language learning support. All of this is intended to be informal, and we encourage you to take your time so that you can develop your understanding of the key skills and apply them. At times, you may find some of the tasks and questions challenging, but please don't worry, this is fine. One way to improve is to stretch yourself – to try some harder tasks. If you are finding something difficult, you can seek help: ask a parent or a friend to support you. It's fine in the practice units to work through them at your own pace, with help where needed, and to look again at areas to understand them better.

At the end of the book, we offer formal examination practice. This should be approached differently. We suggest you approach these papers as 'mock' exams. In other words, follow the times set out for each exam paper as stated on the front page. Take these exams in a quiet location where you will not be disturbed, and where it feels like exam-room conditions.

Knowledge comes first. Each of the main skills units starts with a Knowledge section. For English as a Second Language, the knowledge does not refer to any specific content. It refers to what you need to know about the approach taken to improve in each of the four main skills of reading, writing, listening, and speaking.

In the Recap sections you are reminded of the key skills that you need to focus on and improve that will help you be successful in the examinations. The 'What does this mean for you?' sections explain the skills and sub-skills so that you understand how you are assessed.

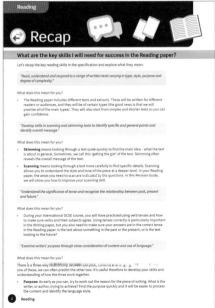

Reflect

In each Reflect section a table allows you to keep a record of your skills level before, and after, each of the four practice units. In other words, you can track your progress.

Apply

Once you are happy with the knowledge and skills you need, you can move to the final stage: Apply (or Practice). In each unit, each of the main parts of the examination paper is broken down and analysed. For each examination task, the 'What do we notice about …?' sections help prepare you further for specific texts, tasks, and question types. When you have completed all of the Apply sections in the four main practice units, you will have practised answering the full range of question types for all four examinations.

Throughout the four main practice units, you will find special feature panels containing guidance, support, tips, and feedback to help you. These are outlined below.

Key Points

Key points help you understand the structure of each of the parts of the examination so you are clear about what to do and how to answer each question type.

Language Support

For all four skills, there is language support that helps improve, for example, your grammar, punctuation, vocabulary, and use of tenses, whether you are reading, writing, speaking, or listening. Language support includes examples of idioms and common expressions to help you use more natural English.

Exam Tip

Exam tips are useful pointers to help you understand better how you are being assessed. They explain aspects of certain types of questions – for example multiple choice questions (MCQs) – so that you are well-prepared. Tips are of a broader, wider nature and aim to boost your confidence before you start to answer exam-style questions.

Examiner Input

These features differ from exam tips as they are more precise and relate to specific questions. For example, they guide you on what you should do for a certain question type, and also what you should not do or should avoid doing. Think of this input as an examiner giving you hints as you attempt the questions.

Examiner Feedback

Once you have attempted each section, you can look at the examiner feedback. The answers to questions are given in these sections and you are shown why each answer is correct. In many cases, you are also shown why alternative answers are not correct and, where relevant, you are provided with sample answers which will be marked as correct. For example, in cases where you are answering questions using your own words.

Rephrasing

In the Reading unit, this feature is used to help you understand a question by looking at it in a different way, perhaps by using alternative words or phrasing.

Revision Tip

Each revision tip helps you to prepare for a specific text or task by suggesting work you can do of a similar nature in the weeks before the examinations. These are not intended as 'night before the exam' reminders! Allow yourself the time to carry out these revision suggestions. Some suggestions will focus on improving specific skills – for example, how best to revise for the Speaking test, or some suitable recordings you can listen to towards improving specific listening skills.

Answers are provided for you in this book. This is because we want you to work through each main task, and each of the question types using the examiner feedback. We recommend that you take in all of the advice and tips offered to help you with each task, have a go at answering each question, and then look up the answers and read the examiner feedback.

The practice papers at the back of the book are different as they do not contain any advice, guidance, tips, or feedback. The unit is meant to be formal practice for each of the four examinations.

⚙ Knowledge

What do I need to know about the Reading paper?

The examination will not test your knowledge of specific content. However, the extracts and the questions will relate to the themes and topics set out in the specification. In the Reading paper, you will engage with all of the themes and topics. This is also referred to as 'subject content', and the three themes are:

Theme one – Identity and culture

Theme two – Local, national, international and global areas of interest

Theme three – Current and future study and employment.

You are expected to understand and identify information, ideas, and opinions about these themes relating to the experiences of other people, including people in countries and communities where English is a main language.

You need to know:

- the structure of the Reading paper, so that you are fully prepared for the examination and there will be no surprises

- the themes and topics that are in the specification, which will help you predict what to expect in the Reading texts

- the range of question types and how you are expected to write down your answers and responses

- how you will be assessed by the examiners – in other words, where you will gain marks and how best to optimise this to raise your grade.

You will develop your understanding by working through practice questions and reading the relevant features like those listed in the 'How to use this book' section on pages v–vi.

Assessment objectives: Reading

Understand and respond to written language

R1: Identify and select relevant detail, key points and ideas.

R2: Show understanding of vocabulary, ideas and purpose.

R3: Collate, organise and present relevant detail.

R4: Draw inferences, make deductions, and recognise implicit meaning.

Recap

What are the key skills I will need for success in the Reading paper?

Let's recap the key reading skills in the specification and explore what they mean:

"Read, understand and respond to a range of written texts varying in type, style, purpose and degree of complexity."

What does this mean for you?

- The Reading paper includes different texts and extracts. These will be written for different readers or audiences, and they will be of certain types (the good news is that we will practise all of the main types). They will also start from simpler and shorter texts so you can gain confidence.

"Develop skills in scanning and skimming texts to identify specific and general points and identify overall message."

What does this mean for you?

- **Skimming** means looking through a text quite quickly to find the main idea – what the text is about in general. Sometimes, we call this 'getting the gist' of the text. Skimming often reveals the overall message of the text.

- **Scanning** means looking through a text more carefully to find specific details. Scanning allows you to understand the style and tone of the piece at a deeper level. In your Reading paper, the areas you need to scan are indicated by the questions. In this *Revision Guide*, we will show you how to improve your scanning skill.

"Understand the significance of tense and recognise the relationship between past, present and future."

What does this mean for you?

- During your International GCSE course, you will have practised using verb tenses and how to make sure verbs and their subjects agree. Using tenses correctly is particularly important in the Writing paper, but you also need to make sure your answers are in the correct tense in the Reading paper. Is the text about something in the past or the present, or is the text looking to the future?

"Examine writers' purpose through close consideration of content and use of language."

What does this mean for you?

There is a three-way relationship between purpose, content, and language. When we know one of these, we can often predict the other two. It's useful therefore to develop your skills and understanding of how the three work together.

- **Purpose:** As early as you can, try to work out the reason for the piece of writing. What is the writer, or author, trying to achieve? Find the purpose quickly and it will be easier to process the content and identify the language style.

- **Content:** This will vary from text to text, so it's important that your skimming skill identifies quickly what the text is about – its content. You can think of content as the details, the facts, the dates/times, etc.

- **Language:** A writer will have chosen language that is appropriate for the content. It's important therefore to recognise where a specific style of language and certain language devices, or tools, have been used. You will be tested regularly in your Reading paper on the effect and interpretation of language.

"Explore what is implied but not actually stated and make appropriate inference and deduction."

What does this mean for you?

This is a higher order skill. In English, we use LOTS and HOTS: lower order (LO) and higher order (HO) thinking skills (TS). The first text in your Reading paper is designed to practise your LOTS. However, as you work through the paper, you will be asked to show higher order skills, and this means practising and developing two particular skills:

- **Inference:** A writer may imply something rather than state it as fact – in other words suggest rather than explain. Rather than telling you exactly what has happened or is happening, the writer will give clues or hints so that you can work out what is really going on. With inference, you are given some hints, and you work out as quickly as you can what is meant. This is sometimes called 'reading between the lines'.

- **Deduction:** This is a similar skill to inference in that the text does not give the meaning as a straightforward explanation, and you have to work out what is meant. With deduction, you have to draw logical conclusions based on the information you have been given.

Reflect

Reflecting on my current reading skills

Complete the table below right now with an estimate of your current reading skills. Just tick the box that you feel is closest to your level. That's all you need to do at the moment. We will return to this later.

Key skills	I think I need to improve in this area	I'm already quite good at this
Identifying a range of the different types of texts and noting the differences between them		
Skimming to get a feel of what the text is about (the gist) and locating the key points and main ideas quickly		
Scanning for a closer look at a text to locate specific details		
Checking the verbs to identify the specific verb tenses and which tense a text as a whole is using		
Identifying the main purpose of a text		
Knowing and using language relating to themes and topics		
Being aware of language devices (tools) – the language skills a writer uses on purpose for effect and to create impact		
Using inference to work out what is meant from clues and hints		
Using deduction to work out what is meant by a logical analysis of the information that is given		

Apply

What is the best way for me to apply this knowledge and these skills to practise for the Reading paper?

Text 1

That's exactly what this *Revision Guide* is here for. Let's start with Text 1, the first extract you will see in the Reading paper.

Common text types

Texts that have featured in previous exams include:

- an email to a friend about holiday plans, and going to a music concert with college friends

- an email to a friend about taking part in a competitive tennis match, followed by a pizza treat afterwards

- an email to a college friend about a part-time job, and a plan to meet at the town library re-opening event after it was damaged by a storm

- an email to a friend that gives information about voluntary work for a global charity that builds pipes to provide clean water, and that tries to convince the friend to take part too

- an email to a friend about a visit from family from Canada, and some advice needed to replace a broken laptop with a new one.

What do we notice about Text 1?

The content can vary but the text is meant to help you start the exam confidently. Texts that are likely to be used:

- an email in two parts.

What are the key assessment elements of Text 1?

Marks available	Number of words	How I will gain marks
6 marks – 6 questions	200–250 words	• by identifying and selecting relevant detail, key points and ideas (R1) • by showing understanding of vocabulary, ideas and purpose (R2)

Now let's look at an example of Text 1 and the types of questions you are likely to be asked.

Read the first part of this email from Tong to Lucy.

Dear Lucy

1 I am back in Thailand now, but I had a wonderful time in England when I was with your family for a week. The room your parents gave me was perfect. They were very kind to put me on the second floor of the apartment, which had such a nice view.

2 My home is in Bangkok and the view from my bedroom is of high-rise buildings. It's very different to the view from your guest room, of trees and the park. Our apartment is on the 26th floor, so I can also see the busy roads and the city trains above the roads. What a contrast!

Key Points

Note how the email is split into two parts. The second part has a different focus. Questions 01–03 are based on the first part of the email, which is about Tong's rooms in England and Thailand. Each question is worth 1 mark.

Assessment Objectives

R1, R2. You will not be asked to collate or organise material. You only need to select what is relevant to the questions and to show your understanding.

Exam-style questions

Let's explore questions 01 to 03, which relate to the first part of the email.

01 On what floor of the apartment did Tong stay? Write the correct letter in the box.

A	The ground floor
B	The first floor
C	The second floor

[1 mark]

02 What can Tong see from his room in Bangkok? Write the correct letter in the box.

A	A park
B	Buildings
C	Trees

[1 mark]

03 What is the **main** point of **paragraph 2**? Write the correct letter in the box.

A	To compare Tong and Lucy's schools
B	To compare Tong's and Lucy's parents
C	To compare the locations of the two apartments

[1 mark]

Exam Tip

Notice how the question uses a different word – 'stay' – to ask about where Tong slept. The word 'room' is used in the email. You don't need to infer, but you do need to do some processing rather than just copy or 'lift' the word from the text. Look for the key words in a text that the question links to.

Examiner Input

Be sure to write your answer in the box supplied underneath the options. You will need to write the letter or letters – for example, A. Do **not** use a tick.

Examiner Input

Question 03 asks you to show you understand the main point of a paragraph. By main point it means what the paragraph is mainly focusing on – its central idea.

Read the second part of the email.

3   I'm sorry I wasn't much of a help to you when we played tennis against your parents. To be honest, it's not my favourite sport and I'm not very good at it. My parents really enjoy playing badminton in Bangkok, but sadly I don't enjoy that either. I like my football.

4   Last week, I went to play badminton with my mother and father for the first time in a very long time. The people here prefer to play in large open buildings at a very warm temperature of about 30°C. Not like your local sports centre, which was quite cool, and air-conditioned.

5   Playing tennis with your parents and playing badminton with mine has helped me realise that family time is important and that sports can help bring us closer together.

Tong

 Language Support

Expressions

'for the first time in a very long time': A 'very long time' is likely to be a period of months or even years – try to work out the length of time from the context. We can infer that Tong has not played badminton with his parents for many months.

Let's explore questions 04 to 06, which relate to the second part of the email.

04 Which sport does Tong enjoy taking part in? Write the correct letter in the box.

A	Badminton
B	Football
C	Tennis

[1 mark]

 **Exam Tip**

Look out for answers that can be proven not to be true based on information given in the extract. For example, Answers A and C can be proven not to be true, so Answer B must be the correct one.

05 In Bangkok, which conditions do people like in order to enjoy playing badminton? Write the correct letter in the box.

A	Cool
B	Dry
C	Hot

[1 mark]

Exam Tip

Questions and answers on the Reading paper might sometimes use negatives. Look out for this. For example, question 04 could have been, "Which sport does Tong not enjoy playing?"

Rephrasing

Sometimes, you can work out the correct answer by looking for **synonyms** – words with the same or similar meaning. Look for a synonym for 'like' from question 05. How about 'prefer'?

Language Support

It's good to revise your semantic fields – words that are related to each other. For example, words used to describe the weather include: hot, humid, cold, frozen, icy, wet, rainy, stormy, windy, foggy, thunderous. Maybe you can think of some more?

06 What is the **main** purpose of the email? Write the correct letter in the box.

A	To remember that sport can be an activity which is good for families
B	To complain about Tong's life in Bangkok
C	To suggest ways that Tong can improve his badminton skills

[1 mark]

Revision Tip

You could ask your friends or family if you can read their informal emails (for example, emails to friends and family members). If the emails are about 200 words long, then that is great. Try to establish the purpose of the email, and then look at any specific details. To revise, you could also write your own email to a friend in the same format as Text 1. Then try setting your own multiple-choice questions. Share these with a partner who is also taking the International GCSE ESL examination.

Examiner feedback and raising my grade

How well did you do on Text 1? There are 6 marks available. Check your answers with the correct answers below. Note the feedback from the examiner to help you understand why a particular answer is correct and why some alternative answers are not correct.

Examiner Input

For multiple-choice questions (MCQs), try not to predict any patterns, for example A, B, C, A, B, C. This is not how the questions are set. However, it is unlikely that all of the answers will be Answer A. If your answers are all Bs, for example, it would be a good idea to review your answers. It's more likely that some As, some Bs, and some Cs will feature. It's likely that in a series of six MCQs all three (A, B, and C) will feature at least once.

Answers to Text 1

Text 1: An email from Tong to Lucy

Questions 01–06

01   C

Examiner Feedback

Question 01 is a straightforward question, requiring you to 'identify and select' the relevant detail about the floor, or storey, that Tong is staying on. In the UK, the bottom floor of a building is called the 'ground' floor. Internationally, this might be called the first floor. But don't let prior knowledge affect your choice. The text states 'second floor'.

02   B

Examiner Feedback

It is stated in the email that Tong's bedroom has a view of 'high-rise buildings'. Suggested answers A and C contain details from the text and are therefore **distractors**. For more about distractors, see page 22.

03   C

Examiner Feedback

There is no evidence for A – they don't discuss their schools. Answer B is an example of a distractor that seems like a reasonable thing to conclude. However, nothing is said about Tong's parents in paragraph 2 and if you are comparing you would need to have some details to compare with.

04   B

Examiner Feedback

As Tong says, 'I like my football', we know that he enjoys it. Answer A is a distractor as the text suggests that Tong doesn't enjoy playing badminton with his parents. Answer C is also a distractor as in the text Tong states that tennis is 'not my favourite sport'.

05   C

Examiner Feedback

A is the distractor, as it is in England where cool conditions are preferred. There is no evidence for B (dry) so answering B would be making an assumption that along with hot, the air would be dry.

06   A

Examiner Feedback

Answer B lacks evidence from the text to back it up. Tong is not complaining, he is just stating some facts about his home city and his home area. Answer C may well be a purpose that Tong has – to improve. However, there is no evidence in the email of this. Tong just states that he was not very good at tennis. We don't know about his badminton skills.

My score for Text 1	
What I found difficult	
What I have learnt	
Three ways I can improve	• _____ • _____ • _____

Text 2

Now let's turn our attention to Text 2, the second extract you will see in the Reading paper.

Common text types

Texts that have featured in previous exams include:

- a description of a tour of a football club's ground, visitor centre, and café
- a description of the duties of a job caring for animals and liaising with the public
- an account of how plastic bags cause pollution and threaten sea life, and how this can be reduced
- a talk by a student about his hero – his grandfather
- a recipe from a blog, and how to cook a pasta sauce meal.

What do we notice about Text 2?

Texts that might also be used include:

- advertisements and public information bulletins, providing specific information
- the text of a speech – persuasive speeches and speeches that give information or advice.

What are the key assessment elements of Text 2?

Marks available	Number of words	How I will gain marks
12 marks – usually 8 questions	400–500 words	• by identifying and selecting relevant detail, key points and ideas (R1) • by showing understanding of vocabulary, ideas and purpose (R2) • by collating, organising and presenting relevant detail (R3) • by inferring, making deductions and recognising implicit meaning (R4)

Now let's look at an example of Text 2 and the types of questions you are likely to be asked.

Read the first part of this advertisement about a trip to India.

---

1 **Become a blogger in India**

How would you like to spend a month blogging in India? On a one-month tour that takes in an old city, a modern city, a fabulous building, and a beach. And here's the amazing thing – it's free. This is a sponsored trip, so your costs are covered by our company *Unique Blogs*. However, this opportunity is only available for a short period and we cannot guarantee every applicant a place. It's first come, first served!

2 **Our application process**

Before you apply, be sure that:

- you are a full-time student aged 18 or over
- this is your first trip to India
- you can bring spending money of 200 US dollars
- you have your own tablet or a small laptop
- you agree to keep a daily blog of your experiences that we can use.

3 If you can meet the above requirements, please apply on our website form. Please note that the closing date is the end of October. You can also send us an email.

4 If selected, we will contact you and begin arrangements for your dream trip to India. Please make sure you have a current passport, as we will apply for a student visa on your behalf.

Key Points

Note how the first part of the advertisement includes a bulleted list. Lists may or may not appear in the exam text, but it is sensible for you to be prepared for a list. If there is a list, there is likely to be a question that focuses on information within it. Remember that you can use the key words and phrases from a list – you don't have to write down the full sentence or line.

Assessment Objectives

R1, R2, R3, R4. In addition to the R1 and R2 assessment objectives tested in Text 1, you will be tested on your skills to collate, organise, and present relevant detail (R3) and infer, deduce, and recognise implicit meaning (R4).

Exam-style questions

Let's explore questions 07 to 10, which relate to the first part of Text 2.

 Examiner Input

For questions that require you to write on answer lines, you don't need to fill up all of the space. For example, this answer only requires one or two words. An examiner will award the mark if the relevant detail is there and the words show clear understanding of the question.

Answer questions **07** to **10**.

07 How long will a successful applicant spend in India?　　　**[1 mark]**

_____

08 Why is it important to apply for this opportunity quickly?

Write the correct letter in the box.

A	It guarantees acceptance.
B	It's a first come, first served opportunity.
C	The cost is lower for early applicants.

[　]

[1 mark]

 Exam Tip

You can practise modelling your answers by looking for the question word. In this question, it is why – so you are looking for a reason, or an explanation. Other question words include: what, where, who, which, how, how many.

09 Read the following. Which **two** statements are correct?

Write the correct letters in the boxes.

A	You must be in full-time study.
B	You live in India.
C	You will be provided with a computer.
D	You agree to the *Unique Blogs* company making use of your blog.

[　] [　]

[2 marks]

 Exam Tip

You are likely to see a question such as this, which asks you to look at statements and decide which are true and which are false. For question 09, also note that you need to choose two true statements, for 1 mark each. Always read questions carefully and be sure of what you have to do and/or provide. This is time well spent.

10 Which **two** ways can someone apply for this opportunity? [2 marks]

1 _____

2 _____

✎ Rephrasing

Some questions do not use question words, but ask you to find items using phrases such as 'give two ways', 'name two things', 'list two advantages', and so on. You will be provided with separate lines for each item. Practise changing the wording of these questions to make them easier to understand.

You could also rephrase the whole question if that helps. For example: 'What are two methods I can use to apply?'

Now read the second part of this text, which focuses on four specific locations that the student will visit in India.

5 Two cities

We will take you to Bangalore – India's modern centre of information technology – where hundreds of companies have created millions of jobs for technology engineers. 40% of India's IT industry is located in Bangalore. Later, you will visit Varanasi, one of the oldest inhabited cities in the world dating back 2800 years. Here, you will see ancient crafts and customs being practised by people as they have been since the dawn of time.

6 The Taj Lake Palace Hotel

In the 19th century, the royal palace was in a poor condition. In the 1960s, the building was redeveloped and was turned into a luxury hotel. The American architect Didi Contractor was the designer. In its glory days – 50 years ago – the building had visits from well-known guests including Jacqueline Kennedy and Queen Elizabeth II. However, its most famous moment occurred in 1983, when it was used for a *James Bond* movie. The hotel can only be reached by its guests using a private boat service across the lake. However, we have a special arrangement in place for you to pay a visit.

7 Beach life in Chennai

We will take you to Marina Beach in Chennai. Marina Beach is the second-longest beach in the world, and the longest in India. The beach is mostly sandy, and the beach front has souvenir shops and local vendors selling fresh food for your final taste of India, such as crispy sundal – a protein-rich dry mixture of chickpeas, coconut, and mustard seeds. The beach is your last excursion before you leave India.

Revision Tip

Note that the second part of the advertisement is mostly factual and the first part was mostly instructions. This is the approach generally taken for Text 2. To revise for Text 2, you should look at texts that are about 400–450 words that have instructions and/or a factual, informative basis.

Let's explore questions 11 to 14, which relate to the second part of Text 2.

---

11 In **paragraph 5**, the writer says 'since the dawn of time'.

Explain in your own words what this phrase means.   **[1 mark]**

_____

_____

_____

_____

 **Exam Tip**

If you do not know the meaning of an idiom or phrase, context clues can help you. Look at the full sentence that includes 'since the dawn of time' and you will see the word 'ancient'. Further back, you will see 'oldest inhabited cities'. These two clues should help you understand the context.

Language Support

Proverbs and idioms will feature in the Reading paper texts and also in the spoken English you will hear during the Listening paper. A **proverb** is a short saying that states a truth as a piece of general advice. An **idiom** is an expression that cannot be understood from the meanings of its separate words – so it must be learnt as a whole. Examples:

Travel proverb: *A day of travelling will bring a basketful of learning.* (Vietnamese)

Travel idiom: My work as a global sales director means I'm *living out of a suitcase*.

Language Support

'Glory days' is an idiom and it means a period of time when something or someone was popular and highly successful. For example: the glory days of Manchester United football club were more than 20 years ago when they were winning trophies.

 Revision Tip

More about idioms

'Since the dawn of time' is also an idiom. Many idioms used in English have the word 'time' in them. Examples, with their meanings:

* *behind the times* – not aware of or not using the latest ideas or techniques
* too much *time on my hands* – to have extra or spare time with nothing specific to do
* I wish I could *turn back time* – I wish I could go back to the past and change an action for the better
* *the time is right* – the most suitable time to do something
* *living on borrowed time* – to be in a temporary position, which is likely to come to an end sooner rather than later.

You can do an internet search using 'idioms about time' and make a list of the common ones.

12 Read **paragraph 6**.

Which **two** statements are correct?

Write the correct letters in the boxes.

A	The hotel has always been in an excellent condition.
B	The hotel was restored with the help of an American architect.
C	The hotel has been the scene of a famous film.
D	The hotel on the lake can be reached by a bridge.

[2 marks]

(!) Exam Tip

Look carefully at Statement D. It gives a means of getting to the island that is not in the main text. What is it? A bridge. As a general piece of advice, you should focus only on the information in a text. If a question adds information that is not in the text and is not relevant, you can ignore it. In other words, make sure that your answers come from the text and can be found (evidenced) in the text or inferred from it.

✎ Rephrasing

Providing a list of statements for you to check which ones are correct is a common approach in the Reading paper. The answers will usually have a 'stem', that is a main word or words from the paragraph. In the answers to question 12, the stem is 'The hotel'. In question 12, Statement A says that the hotel has always been in an excellent condition. Or maybe it has not? Try rephrasing the statement to give the opposite meaning. This approach might help you to be clearer about whether a fact is correct or not. For example, rephrase Statement C to 'The hotel either has or has not been the scene of a film'.

◎ Language Support

Note that Statements B and C in question 12 both use synonyms – words that have the same or similar meanings. See if you can spot the synonyms for 'restored' and 'film' in the main text. A good knowledge of synonyms is recommended for success.

(!) Exam Tip

It's a good idea to forget what you know about a topic and only focus on the information in the text that you are given. It is your ability to identify information in a text that is being tested and not how much you know about a particular topic. It is tempting to use your own prior knowledge of a topic – maybe you have already been to the Taj Lake Palace Hotel – but do not be tempted. Use only the information or content of the text or extract.

13 Read **paragraph 7**.

Which **two** statements are correct?

Write the correct letters in the boxes.

A	The beach is the second-longest in India.
B	The beach is not sandy.
C	The beach has places you can buy snacks to eat.
D	The beach is your last visit.

[2 marks]

14 What is the **main** purpose of the text?

Write the correct letter in the box.

A	To inform the reader about ancient India
B	To appeal for suitable people to go on a trip to India
C	To discuss tourism in India

[1 mark]

 Exam Tip

Statement A is not correct because the text states that Marina Beach is the longest beach in India. Statement B is given to you in the negative, so be on the lookout for this. In the text, we read that the beach is 'mostly sandy' so we can infer that Statement B is wrong.

 Language Support

Remember what you have just practised regarding synonyms. The synonyms you need to identify to answer question 13 are 'snacks' and 'visit'.

 Language Support

When you are asked about the purpose of a text as a whole, you will be given choices using verbs such as advise, persuade, explain, describe, inform, discuss, and tell. This can help you to find the correct statement and purpose. Explaining is different from discussing, and describing is different from persuading. If you are confident of the purpose of the writing, then you will understand the questions about it better. For example, is the advertisement for a trip to India to complain, to appeal, or to advise? Yes, the main purpose is to appeal to students so they apply.

Revision Tip

At or towards the end of the questions about Text 2, you are likely to be asked about its main purpose. Hopefully, you will have thought about this as you skimmed the text the first time. Go back and skim the text again. Now that you have answered all of the questions, do you see the main purpose – or the gist – of the text clearly? Locate some texts that are similar to the length and type that are often used for Text 2. Search for them on the internet using some key words from the 'What do we notice about Text 2?' section on page 10. Read the texts quickly and write down in a sentence what the gist of the text is. You could show the text and your sentence to someone else and compare what they write down.

 Exam Tip

It is the main purpose of the text that is required in question 14. That means you need to look at the text as a whole and decide what the writer is trying to achieve overall. Think about how the text has been organised and how the relevant detail has been presented. Texts will also have lesser purposes: for example, this text also describes a beach and how we can enjoy it, but that is not the main purpose.

Examiner feedback and raising my grade

How well did you do in Text 2? There are 12 marks available. Check your answers with the correct answers below. Note the feedback from the examiner to help you understand why a particular answer is correct and why some alternative answers are not correct.

Answers to Text 2

Text 2: Advertisement about a trip to India

Questions 07–13

07	One month/1 month/a month/month

Examiner Feedback

If you wrote, 'It will be a one-month journey' this would not be allowed because it's not a close enough response. A note about mark schemes: if you see the forward slash, /, it means it is a similar answer and it will be accepted.

08	B

Examiner Feedback

A is wrong because acceptance is not guaranteed. C is also wrong as the costs are covered fully by the organisation (there is no cost to the applicant).

09	A and D

Examiner Feedback

A is correct because 'full-time student' is the same as 'full-time study'. D is correct because the advertisement says that you must allow the company to use your blog. Note that B is wrong as this has to be a first trip to India, so living in India makes this incorrect. C is also wrong as the fourth criteria states you need to bring your own computer or tablet.

10	The two ways are:

- Complete a website form
- Send an email

Examiner Feedback

If you answered 'website' for one of the ways, it will not be enough detail. 'Website form' is needed. If you answered 'Send us an email' then this is accepted. When providing details from a list in the text, it's always best to include as much detail as you feel confident to include. Alternative correct answers would be: By using the form on our website. By sending us an email.

11 From the beginning of time

Examiner Feedback

Look at the full sentence from the text: 'Here you will see ancient crafts and customs being practised by people as they have been since the dawn of time.' The idiom – since the dawn of time – is used to show that the local people have been following their crafts and customs for a very long time indeed and it is your understanding of this that is being tested. Other ways you could state this using your own words are:

- For thousands of years
- From the beginning of their people/from the start of their culture
- For ever/always
- For ages.

The examiner will want to see that you have understood the concept, so if you answered 'from the dawn of the day as the sun rose' it would not be correct.

12 B and C

Examiner Feedback

A: It is clear from the first sentence that the hotel has not always been in good condition, as it was in a poor condition two centuries ago.

B: Yes, and the synonyms are 'restored' and 'redeveloped'.

C: Yes, it was the scene (or 'set') of a famous *James Bond* film. Note another synonym here – 'film' for 'movie'.

D: The hotel cannot be reached via a bridge. There is no evidence of a bridge in the text. It can, however, be reached by a boat, which is evidenced in the text.

13 C and D

Examiner Feedback

A: This is incorrect: the text states that the beach is the longest in India (see the second sentence in paragraph 7).

B: The text states that the beach is 'mostly sandy', so it is not true to state that it is not sandy. Remember to look out for questions and statements that use the negative.

C: Yes, you can buy a delicious sundal, so yes, you can buy food. Snacks are food.

D: Yes, the beach will be the last day trip – the 'last excursion' ('day trip' and 'excursion' are synonyms). Other synonyms you should learn are: trip, outing, expedition, tour, jaunt. However, they don't all have exactly the same meanings, so try to learn the subtle differences. Not all synonyms are equal.

14   B

Examiner Feedback

Answer A is not correct as the text also focuses on modern India. Whilst there is mention of ancient India this is not the main focus. Answer C states that tourism is discussed. However, there is no analysis, review, or consideration of tourism.

My score for Text 2	
What I found difficult	
What I have learnt	
Four ways I can improve	• _____ • _____ • _____ • _____

Text 3

Now let's turn our attention to Text 3, the third extract you will see in the Reading paper.

Common text types

Texts that have featured in previous exams include:

- a sustained argument that children in the UK go to school at a much younger age than children in other European countries – and that this causes longer term damage

- a study suggesting that teenagers spend too much time on smartphones and social media – and that they should reflect on this to reduce the time spent

- an account of a new employee starting a job in London for a media company – and a kind-natured colleague who helped the employee get through the first week

- advice for a first-year student of what to take when moving away from home to go to university, focusing on setting up their room, food and drink, study needs, and clothing

- advice from a careers consultant about how to ensure you apply for a job that matches your personality and skills – and factors that make people happy at work to ensure a good work-life balance.

What do we notice about Text 3?

Texts that are likely to be used:

- might be an extract from a brochure, letter, newspaper, magazine, or specialised website

- might be a transcript of a talk that sets out to persuade a point of view

- usually contain opinions

- can be written in the first, second, or third person

- feature topics that allow opinions, advice, and guidance to be offered, such as the age children start school, over-reliance on social media, starting a new job, first year at university, and ensuring job satisfaction

- are all non-fiction texts containing some facts, details, examples, and views expressed by others

- tend to be structured in paragraph form using full sentences and if lists are used, they are likely to be set out as sentences

- can vary in length and number of words: a shorter text might be 400 words, but you should also plan for texts of up to 600 words.

What are the key assessment elements of Text 3?

Marks available	Number of words	How I will gain marks
18 marks – the number of questions can vary and has been between 7 and 10 questions on previous exam papers	400–600 words	• by identifying and selecting relevant detail, key points and ideas (R1) • by showing understanding of vocabulary, ideas and purpose (R2) • by collating, organising and presenting relevant detail (R3) • by inferring, making deductions and recognising implicit meaning (R4)

Now let's look at an example of Text 3 and the types of questions you are likely to be asked.

Read the first part of the article about how some coffee shops function also as workspaces.

1 **Where can I grab a coffee?**

Coffee shops are so much more these days than places that only serve drinks. They open early at 9am and you can still pop in for a late morning coffee about 10am as it starts to get busy. By 11am you are likely to be surrounded by many people who are not merely enjoying a drink. When it's that packed, I just want to exclaim loudly, "Go and work from home, please!"

2 **Coffee and work**

Many coffee shops are now work zones. They come complete with wifi, and plug-ins for laptops, tablets, and smartphones. This is more so in major cities, where there are more people working on a flexible basis. Some are likely to be WFH – working from home – but they say that they feel more inspired with others around them. Others are self-employed and are carrying out their work projects from the coffee shop.

3 *Office Coffee* is a newly opened shop in the Old Town area of Dubai. After a brief visit last week, I spoke to their manager and he said "We provide large square tables that colleagues can share as workspaces. The appearance is of an office, but it feels more like your own lounge at home. Our coffee is delicious – we use only the best imported Italian blends. We serve a great breakfast as people work. Our wifi is free and unlimited. All in all, we cater very well for the working professionals."

4 I noticed that this coffee shop also has allocated individual corner seats for people to concentrate on their work. They can also sit at one of the raised window seats, where they can take their time and perhaps watch the people going about their business outside. Mind you, from what I have seen, without necessarily doing any work.

Key Points

This text uses subheadings. This is a common feature in Text 2, but can also feature in Text 3. Subheadings help you navigate through the text as you read. Each subheading in some way relates to the overall theme, but adds a new aspect or a different dimension. As you read on, you will discover that this text is about different types of coffee shops.

Other examples of Text 3 may not have any subheadings, but instead might be made up of about 6–8 paragraphs. You can then look for the topic sentences, as they are likely to hint at the overall message in a paragraph. With Text 3 above, look at the opening line and note how it hints at what is to come. The topic of the first paragraph is how coffee shops offer so much more now than they used to (in the view of the writer). We can define a topic sentence as expressing the main idea in the paragraph. Be careful, however, as not all paragraphs use topic sentences.

Assessment Objectives

R1, R2, R3, R4. As with Text 2, Text 3 tests your skills in all four areas.

Exam-style questions

Let's explore questions 15 to 18, which relate to the first part of the article.

15 Read **paragraph 1**.

Which statement is correct?

Write the correct letter in the box.

A	Coffee shops open before 9am.
B	Coffee shops are quiet places at 10am.
C	Coffee shops are busy places at 11am.

[1 mark]

16 What is the **main** point of **paragraph 2**?

Write the correct letter in the box.

A	To describe how coffee shops are places where people often work
B	To represent an average working person
C	To illustrate how technologically advanced coffee shops are now

[1 mark]

17 In **paragraph 3**, the writer gives information about *Office Coffee*, a newly opened coffee shop.

Which **four** details are correct?

Write the correct letters in the boxes.

A	The writer visited the coffee shop twice in the previous week.
B	The coffee shop has square tables to be used by customers.
C	The workspaces feel mostly like an office environment does.
D	The workspaces try to recreate a home environment.
E	Local blends of coffee are preferred.
F	Eating and working is not allowed in *Office Coffee*.
G	There are no extra costs for using the coffee shop's wifi.
H	Professional working people are accommodated.

[4 marks]

> **(!) Exam Tip**
>
> You are likely to have a question which lists 6–8 details from a paragraph, sometimes from two or more paragraphs. This is testing your skill of deduction – looking carefully at the text and deciding which of the details are not correct or not relevant. Look out for details that are not in the text. You can only confirm correct details if the text supports this, that is if you can find evidence in the text. For example, if Statement D was 'The coffee shop serves hot English breakfast tea', you cannot decide this is a correct detail because the text says nothing about serving tea. Perhaps they do, but we don't know this for sure.

18 From **paragraphs 2** and **4**, list **three** things we learn about how a coffee shop can be a good place for people who want to get on with their work? **[3 marks]**

1 _____

_____

_____

2 _____

_____

_____

3 _____

_____

_____

! Exam Tip

You are likely to see a question that asks you to make a list of three or four points. These may be examples, things, or reasons - and you will be directed in the question about what to look for. Some of the items in the text will not be relevant, so it's important to be sure of the specific aspect. For example, in question 18 you are asked to look only at the second and fourth paragraphs, and only for the examples that show that coffee shops are good places to work. In these types of questions, you will be able to narrow it down to a word or a short phrase.

⊚ Language Support

Distractors are details and information in suggested answers that seem close but when you look more deeply are not the answers to the question. The broader meaning of 'distract' is to divert attention away from what is appropriate and relevant. It can help to refer back to the text to help you sort out what might be a distractor in an answer. In question 18, you can scan a specific part of the text (two paragraphs) and locate details that support effective working. Therefore, we can exclude any points that do not relate to effective working, such as:

- there are more coffee shop work zones in major cities
- there are more people working on a flexible basis
- self-employed people do their work there.

You can then ignore any suggested answers that present this information.

Now read the second part of the article, in which the writer visits two themed coffee shops.

5 **Coffee and music**

In Dubai where I live, there are live-music events in many coffee shops in the old town, which locals call 'Old Dubai'. There is a shop in the same street as *Office Coffee* that serves beautiful Arabic coffees, but the real purpose is to sell the music made by local artists. If you happen to be there on a Monday or Wednesday afternoon, you will see a local band perform between 1pm to 3pm. On Fridays, you would need to be there at 2–4pm.

6 In the early evenings, the shop takes on a different atmosphere as it becomes a free 'open mic' place with no costs involved for musicians. On the 'open mic' evening, performers are invited to bring along their guitar, or small keyboard, and sing their own songs. They only have one rule: it must be original music written by the artist. I often go along to listen to the musicians – it's great to see that local artists can enjoy a free venue to air their new songs.

7 Coffee and books

Another coffee shop has opened in a different part of Old Dubai, which looks like a cross between a library and a regular coffee shop. As you sit down, you are surrounded by shelves of books. You can choose a book and read whilst you sip your coffee, and there are children's books also, so families can spend time there. They have a policy – any book can be taken home, as long as you return the favour.

8 I really enjoy these two themed coffee shops, where people can go and mix their coffee drinking with hobbies and leisure. What I don't approve of is coffee shops as replacement office spaces.

Language Support

Notice that in the first sentence of paragraph 5 the word 'live' appears twice. The two words are spelled the same, but mean completely different things. The first 'live' is a verb that means 'to make a home in a particular place'. We know therefore that the writer lives in Dubai. One synonym is 'reside', so the writer resides in Dubai. The second 'live' is an adjective that describes a presentation at which the performers and audience are both present, for example a live show, a live recording, or a live event. The two words are not homonyms as they are not pronounced the same way. Homonyms are words that are spelled the same and sound the same when spoken, but have different meanings.

Let's explore questions 19 to 23, which relate to the second part of the article.

19 What is the main aim of the coffee shop as stated in **paragraph 5**? [1 mark]

_____

_____

20 From **paragraph 5**, list two days and times that you could see a local band perform? [2 marks]

1 _____

2 _____

21 In **paragraph 6**, the writer says that local artists 'can enjoy a free venue to air their new songs'.

Explain in your own words what this phrase means. **[2 marks]**

_____

_____

_____

_____

_____

22 In **paragraph 7**, the writer says that 'any book can be taken home as long as you return the favour'.

Explain in your own words what this phrase means. **[2 marks]**

_____

_____

_____

_____

_____

23 Which statement best describes the purpose of the whole article?

Write the correct answer in the box.

A	To criticise modern coffee shops in Dubai
B	To describe different types of coffee shops in Dubai
C	To promote Arabic and Italian coffee blends in Dubai

[box]

[1 mark]

(!) Exam Tip

There will be several questions on the Reading paper that ask you to use your own words to explain the meaning of a phrase. For these questions, look at the key words within the text and try to find synonyms for those words. If you are unsure what a word means, you can use context clues from the surrounding text to help you. As a hint – the two key words in question 21 are 'free' and 'air', and both of their meanings can be worked out using context clues in the paragraph. We can work out that the venue is free from here: 'as it becomes a free 'open mic' place with no costs involved'. We can work out what air means from here: 'local artists can enjoy a free venue to play in front of an audience and air their new songs'.

(Q) Examiner Input

Your language skills – writing and grammar – are not being closely tested on the Reading paper. You are marked for reading only, so you need not worry about your writing style as long as what you are intending to communicate makes sense in reference to the question, and is in the correct tense. Always check your short answers to make sure they are clear and that the points you make can be easily understood.

Revision Tip

Find some articles from brochures, newspapers, magazines, blogs, or specialised websites that set out to persuade the reader of a point of view, including having strong opinions. Practise recognising any detail or information that takes you away from the main point – that distracts and diverts your attention away. Those details may be interesting, but are unlikely to be part of any questions you are asked if the text featured as a Text 3.

Examiner feedback and raising my grade

How well did you do in Text 3? There are 18 marks available. Check your answers with the correct answers below. Note the feedback from the examiner to help you understand why a particular answer is correct and why some alternative answers are not correct.

Answers to Text 3

Text 3: Article about coffee shops in Dubai

Questions 15–23

| 15 | C |

 Examiner Feedback

A: The writer says that 'They open early at 9am' so we know that they are not open before that, not before 9am but at 9am.

B: At 10am 'it starts to get busy' and this means that it cannot be described as 'quiet'.

| 16 | A |

Examiner Feedback

B is not relevant. It isn't a distractor, as there is no evidence from the paragraph about an average worker. This is information you can ignore, whilst looking for relevant and accurate information.

C is a distractor because it draws you away from the main point made in A. It is relevant because modern technology is mentioned, but it is not the main focus of the paragraph. You can use the topic sentence here to indicate what the rest of the paragraph focuses on.

| 17 | B, D, G, H |

Examiner Feedback

A: The writer visited the coffee shop in the previous week, but only once.

C: The workspaces are described as feeling like someone's home.

E: Actually, Italian blends of coffee are preferred – 'we use only the best imported Italian blends' tells us this.

F: Quite the opposite. Eating whilst working is encouraged, and that's why they serve a breakfast.

| 18 | Any three of the following: |

- Free wifi
- Plug-ins for laptops, tablets, phones/power provided for electric devices such as laptops, tablets, phones
- Inspiration from others who are around/close by
- Individual (allocated) corner seats

Examiner Feedback

A note about mark schemes: if you see the forward slash, /, it means it is a similar answer and it will be accepted. If you see brackets used, ( ), it means that you can include this information, but it is not required to get the mark.

19   Sell music/vinyl records/CDs (made by local artists)

 Examiner Feedback

The main aim of the coffee shop – the 'real purpose' in the text – is to sell music made by local artists. The distractor is that they specialise in Arabic coffees, but that is not their main aim. On the mark scheme, it will be enough for you to just state 'sell music'. Remember that your writing and grammar skills are not being tested, but if you answered 'music sale' that would not be accepted as the meaning is not 'intact', which means that an examiner won't be sure that you have identified the correct answer. Also, if you answered 'sell musical' you will not get a mark, as 'musical' has a different meaning.

20   Any two of the following are needed for 2 marks:
- Monday 1pm to 3pm
- Wednesday 1pm to 3pm
- Friday 2pm to 4pm

Examiner Feedback

Note that on the Reading paper you will not be penalised if you write two correct answers on the same line. However, you should avoid this as it makes it more difficult for the examiner.

The first two responses will be marked if it is a 2-mark question. Always try to write the answers as separate answers on the lines provided.

21   Example answer: Artists have a place to play their music to other people at no cost to themselves.

Examiner Feedback

A maximum of 2 marks is available for question 21.

2 marks: You have explained both the idea of 'free' – at no cost for the musicians – and the idea of 'air' – to sing their songs/play their music/ allow people to hear their music.

1 mark: You have explained only one of the two ideas, or both partially (but not fully).

0 marks: You have not answered correctly or not been able to supply an answer.

Answers will vary, as students need to answer the question in their own words. Here are some other examples of 2–mark answers, so think carefully about why they were given full marks:

- Artists can play their own songs without having to pay the coffee shop.
- The place allows musicians to perform their own music for no fees.
- No fees need to be paid to the venue, so local artists can play their own songs.

Can you work out why the following examples would be given 1 mark?

- Artists can play their own songs and it's free to go and watch them.
- There is no price to pay for a local artist.
- The coffee shop is open mic for free local artists to play their songs.

Hopefully, you worked out that the first answer only covers the free entry for viewers and not that there are no fees for the artists to pay. In the second answer, there is only one idea that is explained – that it is free for the artists. The third answer changes the meaning of the key word 'free'. It suggests that the local artists are free – that is, they have free time available, which is a completely different idea.

22   Example answer: You can take a book home if you bring a book from home back to the shop.

Examiner Feedback

You need to show the examiner that you have understood these two ideas: a book can be taken (from the shop) but that you must (bring a book back to) replace it.

A maximum of 2 marks is available.

2 marks: You have explained both the idea of 'as long as' – provided that you do it – and the idea of 'return the favour' – to do the same in return.

1 mark: You have explained only one of the two ideas, or both partially (but not fully).

0 marks: You have not answered correctly or not been able to supply an answer.

Note that there is a single word that states exactly the same idea as 'returning a favour' – 'reciprocate'.

23   B

 Examiner Feedback

A: Whilst the writer does not approve of coffee shops being used as workplaces, this does not dominate the whole article. There is much more detail about the positive aspects of how coffee shops are offering more than just coffee and snacks. When deciding on your answer for the question about a whole text, remember to look for balance. Skimming will help, as you should be able to get the gist if you look at the text quickly.

C: Yes, these blends are mentioned in a positive way but to promote means to do more than just mention in passing – it means to try to increase sales and awareness, and to actively encourage. This doesn't happen in the article.

My score for Text 3	
What I found difficult	
What I have learnt	
Five ways I can improve	• _____ • _____ • _____ • _____ • _____

Text 4

We can now look at Text 4, the fourth and final passage you will see in the Reading paper.

Common text types

Texts that have featured in previous exams include:

- a first-person narrative about a traveller who is running out of water in China and is heading towards a lake in the distance
(non-fiction because it describes a region of China in a factual way)

- a first-person narrative about witnessing silverback and blackback gorillas in Uganda from very close range
(non-fiction because it is a first-person account that describes a realistic scene of gorillas in their natural habitat)

- a third-person account of the importance of cherry blossom in Japanese culture, describing its beauty and splendour, and when and where it is best to enjoy it
(non-fiction because it's a detailed, accurate, and explanatory account of cherry blossom, the impact it has, specific dates when blossom is likely, and two specific locations that are recommended)

- a first-person narrative about journeying by car through Mediterranean towns on a mission to research olive trees
(non-fiction, because it's an account of a true series of events – the journey did take place as research for a book)

- a first-person account of an explorer who had to return home part way through an expedition to Antarctica as he was suffering from frostbite due to the extreme wind-chill conditions
(non-fiction, because it's an account of a real expedition – the first attempt to cross Antarctica during the polar winter).

What do we notice about Text 4?

Text 4 is a 'literary non-fiction text'. But what does this mean? Non-fiction literature often has a serious point to make, for example about culture. It explores feelings and reactions to interesting, difficult, uplifting things. The quality of the writing is elevated, which means it has similar features to literary fiction, except that it is about real things. The literary features that have been used in previous texts include:

- similes and metaphors

- sustained use of imagery

- significant emotive and sensory language

- dialogue to heighten the narrative

- use of short sentences for effect, often to increase the tension of the moment

- words and language skills that are used to create mood and atmosphere

- symbolism (when one thing is used to represent another)

- onomatopoeia

- personification

- the addition of details such as anecdotes, which aren't strictly necessary but which help create a story feel (and perhaps anecdotes that are not entirely true).

The narrative viewpoint tends to be first person, and the non-fiction element tends to be a real place or a real journey that is taking place. A prose style of writing is used, with a range of sentence types created for effect. Paragraphs and a continuous text (that can vary in length from 400 to 600 words) is what sets Text 4 apart from the previous three texts. You can think of Text 4 as recounting an event based on real things happening in a real place.

What are the key assessment elements of Text 4?

Marks available	Number of words	How I will gain marks
24 marks – varying number of questions	400–600 words	• by showing understanding of vocabulary, ideas and purpose (R2) • by collating, organising and presenting relevant detail (R3) • by inferring, deducting and recognising implicit meaning (R4)

Assessment Objectives

R2, R3, R4. Text 4 will not test the basic skill of identifying and selecting relevant detail, key points and ideas. Text 4 is a higher-level reading text. As R3 is tested, you will be asked to search across several parts of the text and collate relevant details.

Key Points

The Text 4 passage has a different feel to Texts 1, 2, and 3. A writer is often undertaking an unusual journey in a location which offers plenty of opportunities for descriptive and emotive writing. When you take the Reading paper, we recommend that you read all three of the literary non-fiction passages together, quickly, to note the text's structure and get the gist of the narrative. Given what you learnt in the introduction to this section, what do you notice about this text?

Now let's look at an example of Text 4.

Let's start by skim-reading all three extracts (pages 31, 32, and 34). Once you have done this, look at the notes below.

Notes on Text 4

1   It is a first-person narrative written by someone who spends 24 hours at an airport in London.

2   Heathrow Airport and its terminals are real.

3   It is approximately 550 words long.

4   It uses some literary features such as:

- similes (example: as pretty as an airport)

- imagery (examples: crowds, noisy people, stress, people crying or shouting)

- analogy (example: being in the airport is like staying at home from school all day)

- anecdote (example: story about a game played years ago on a shopping trolley).

In the following passage, the writer, Michal Clerizo, describes his experience of spending 24 hours at Heathrow Airport in London whilst not actually travelling anywhere.

Read the first part of the text, which is about the writer's journey to and his arrival at the airport.

1 Unlike my previous journeys, I had not once glanced anxiously at my watch. Time didn't matter. Nor had I constantly performed my usual nervous ritual of fumbling through my pockets, making sure I had my passport, ticket, and credit cards. All that was for people who were actually going somewhere. Me, I was just going to hang out. I didn't even have my passport with me – just a toothbrush, toothpaste, lots of stuff to read, and a notebook and several pens.

2 I arrive at Terminal 4 and head for the airport information desk to pick up a few basic facts. I learn that the first flights land at around 5am and the last arrive at 11pm. The airport itself and some of the shops in the check-in and arrivals area never close, but the trains that run between Terminal 4 and Terminals 1, 2, and 3 stop at 11.45pm.

Exam-style questions

Now let's look at the kinds of questions you could be asked on Text 4.

Let's explore questions 24 and 25, which are based on the first extract.

24 In **paragraph 1** the writer uses the phrase, 'Nor had I constantly performed my usual nervous ritual'.

Explain in your own words what this means.   **[2 marks]**

_____

_____

_____

_____

_____

25 Read **paragraph 1**.

List **four** items the writer regards as important to have with him when he normally travels. **[4 marks]**

1 _____

2 _____

3 _____

4 _____

Now read the second part of the extract, in which the writer spends time in the airport's terminals.

 Language Support

To help you with this extract from the passage, note that by an 'epiphany', the writer means he experiences a moment of suddenly realising something great, or of huge significance to him. Can you see what significant thing he realises?

3 As Douglas Adams observed in *The Long Dark Tea-time of the Soul*, 'It can hardly be a coincidence that no language on earth has ever produced the expression, as pretty as an airport.' My plan is to pass some of my 24 hours searching for something pretty.

4 I'm wandering around again when I have my second epiphany. 'What an idiot I am!' (I'm sure the best epiphanies always begin with that thought.) An airport is a superb place for watching the world come and go. After all, that's exactly what the world is doing at an airport. Except for me – I'm staying put for 24 hours.

5 I survey all four terminals and conclude that check-in areas are crowded, noisy, and full of stress. Arrivals areas are mellower. Terminal 2 has a few rows of comfortable seats over-looking its arrivals area. I sit and observe as people embrace, kiss, cry, or yell down their mobile phones.

6 Hanging around at Heathrow is like staying home from school and spending the entire day in your pyjamas lying on the couch, watching TV, and eating ice cream. (I can't think why it isn't more popular.)

7 A little after midnight, the show ends. As the food shops close, I stock up on provisions for the night. Inside a display case, I see an example of East meeting West – the last doughnut is sitting next to an onion bhaji. I haggle and get the doughnut at half-price.

Let's explore questions 26 to 29, which are based on the second extract.

26 In **paragraph 3**, the writer says, 'My plan is to pass some of my 24 hours searching for something pretty.'

Explain in your own words what this means. **[2 marks]**

_____

_____

_____

_____

27 From **paragraphs 4** and **5** list what the writer concludes about airports.

List **four** things he concludes. **[4 marks]**

1 _____

2 _____

3 _____

4 _____

28 What is the **main** point of **paragraph 6**?

Write the correct letter in the box.

A	To recommend spending a day at an airport but not as a passenger
B	To describe a day off school watching TV
C	To question why staying off school isn't more popular

[   ]

[1 mark]

> **! Exam Tip**
>
> The reading skill of collating, organising, and presenting relevant detail (Assessment Objective R3) is the main skill you demonstrate through answering questions that ask for a list, or a number of examples from a text. Be sure to check that each of your items stand out as separate and different. For question 27, check that each of your answers is a separate thing that the writer observed.

> **! Exam Tip**
>
> Paragraph 6 is very short and only contains one main sentence, and another in brackets. However, both say a lot. The use of an analogy ('is like staying home from school') means the writer doesn't have to give lots of detail about the first thing being compared ('Hanging around at Heathrow'). An analogy is a literary technique.

> **! Exam Tip**
>
> In more challenging questions like question 28, the answer may not be given directly in the text. Instead you have to piece together hints from what is written. For these questions, try highlighting the key words in the question. You can then scan the text, looking for key words, synonyms, or transition words that match the words you have highlighted. This skill is inference and is part of Assessment Objective R4 – 'draw inferences'. In this context, 'draw' means to work out by taking out or extracting.
>
> The key words in question 28 are recommend, describe, question. Remember that inference needs implication. Try to work out what the writer is trying to imply in paragraph 6. Is he just describing, is his purpose to ask a question, or is he making a recommendation?

29 In **paragraph 7** the writer uses the phrase, 'I haggle and get the doughnut at half-price'.

What does this phrase mean?

Write the correct letter in the box.

A	He dislikes the idea of buying the doughnut.
B	He negotiates a good deal.
C	He prefers to eat the onion bhaji.

[1 mark]

Finally, read the third part of the text, about how the writer remembers and relives his past.

8 I feel sleepy. Hoping for an invigorating sugar-rush, I eat the doughnut. It tastes of onion bhaji. Still sleepy, I decide to try some physical exercise: namely pushing a baggage trolley through the tunnels that connect Terminals 1, 2 and 3. Each tunnel has two moving walkways separated by an expanse of polished marble tiles.

9 While navigating the trolley on the tiles, the child in me takes over. Holding on to the trolley, I break into a run. I realise that I am reliving a game I played years ago in shopping mall parking lots. I haven't lost my touch either, because I am still able to judge the best moment to jump onto the back of the trolley and coast to a gentle stop.

Let's explore questions 30 to 33, which are based on the third and final part of Text 4.

30 In **paragraph 8**, the writer says 'Hoping for an invigorating sugar-rush'.

What does this phrase mean?   [1 mark]

_____

_____

_____

Language Support

If you see a 'Why' question, you should look for phrases or words in the text such as 'because', 'for the reason that', 'so', 'as a result' – as these may link to the answer. Review your knowledge of conjunctions, prepositions, and adverbs that express what's about to come next (or what came just before). This will help you understand important explanations and transitions in the text. For example:

- first, second, third …, then, next, after that, finally
- therefore, as a result, consequently
- although, however, but, whilst, even though
- additionally, furthermore, moreover
- if, as long as, unless, until.

31 What is the **main** point of **paragraph 8**?

Write the correct letter in the box.

A	To convey the invigorating feeling of eating food
B	To show that the writer wants to be more active
C	To describe the tunnels that connect the terminals

[ ]

[1 mark]

 Examiner Input

Be careful of prior knowledge here. You may have spent long periods in airports waiting for flights and finding things to do. But remember, as we have already pointed out, you are only being tested on what is in a text and not on what you already know about a subject or a topic.

32 In **paragraph 9** the writer uses the phrase 'the child in me takes over'.

What does this phrase mean?

Write the correct letter in the box.

A	He remembers being taken to shopping malls when he was young.
B	He is as skilful now as he was when he was young.
C	His adult maturity loses out to his childishness.

[ ]

[1 mark]

33 Which statement best describes the whole passage?

Write the correct letter in the box.

A	It covers a day in an airport with some high and low points.
B	It follows the journey made to an airport.
C	It shows how boring an airport is.

[ ]

[1 mark]

Revision Tip

Now that you have a good feel for the types of passages that are used for Text 4, try to do some background reading in preparation. You can focus on accounts of journeys or experiences by people who have used literary features to enhance a real-life experience. A good place to look is travel blogs on the internet, or articles from travel and cultural magazines, which combine travelling with a meaningful experience. However, remember not to worry about content. You don't need to learn information about places and journeys. The important things are: the structure of Text 4, what makes it literary, and the skills you need to respond to the passage.

Examiner feedback and raising my grade

Answers to Text 4

Text 4: First-person narrative about the writer spending 24 hours at Heathrow Airport

Questions 24–33

24 Example answer: Usually he would be worried and keep checking his pockets to be sure he has his passport, ticket, and cards. This time he does not do this because he is not planning to fly anywhere.

Examiner Feedback

A maximum of 2 marks is available.

2 marks: You have explained both the idea of 'Nor had I constantly performed' (this time he did not constantly check he had his passport, ticket, and cards because he was not actually going to fly anywhere), and the idea of 'my usual nervous ritual' (usually he would be worried and would keep checking his pockets).

1 mark: You have explained only one of the two ideas, or both partially (but not fully).

0 marks: You have not answered correctly or not been able to supply an answer.

Answers will vary, as students need to answer the question in their own words. Here are some other examples of 2 marks, so look carefully at why they were given full marks:

- As he was not leaving the airport, he didn't need to worry about having his passport, ticket, and credit cards.

Can you work out why the examples below were given only 1 mark?

- No need to check he had his passport, ticket, and credit cards.

- He wasn't nervous, as he was not travelling further than the airport.

25 Any four of the following:

- Toothbrush
- Toothpaste
- (Lots of) stuff to read
- Notebook
- (Several) pens.

Examiner Feedback

He doesn't need his passport, ticket, or credit cards. If you said 'books' or 'magazines' instead of 'stuff to read', this would be correct. However, if you said just one pen that would not be correct, as he clearly thinks he needs several of them.

26   Example answer: He plans to spend some of his day, but not all, trying to find an example of something that looks nice in the airport.

Examiner Feedback

A maximum of 2 marks is available.

2 marks: You have explained both the ideas ('some of my 24 hours' and 'as pretty as an airport').

1 mark – you have explained only one of the two ideas, or both partially (but not fully).

0 marks – you have not answered correctly or not been able to supply an answer.

Answers will vary, as students need to answer the question in their own words. Here are some other 2-mark answers. Look carefully at why they were given full marks:

- Airports are not beautiful and that's why he needs to focus some of his time on searching for an example.
- Comparing an airport to something that is beautiful doesn't work very well and the writer has to plan his time, rather than just see something nice-looking.

Can you work out why the examples below were given only 1 mark?

- Airports are not beautiful or attractive places to be.
- He will spend the entire day trying to find something nice-looking in the airport.

27   Any four of the following:

- They are good/superb/ideal places to watch the world come and go. OR They are good/superb/ideal places to watch people/people watch.
- They are crowded.
- They are noisy.
- They can be stressful/full of stress.
- Arrivals areas are mellower than check-in areas.
- People show all (sorts of) emotion.

Examiner Feedback

Note that you are asked what the writer concludes about airports, and not just what the writer concludes. For example, if you wrote 'he thinks he is an idiot' this would not be correct as it is a reflection of himself. If you wrote 'he has surveyed all four terminals', then whilst this is correct, the writer is not making a conclusion. He is merely stating a fact about what he has done. Please read the questions for Text 4 very carefully so that you are sure about which specific details you are looking for.

28   A

 Examiner Feedback

B: The paragraph does describe a lazy, relaxed day off school, but the writer is linking those feelings to his experience at the airport, comparing it to a day off.

C: There is an implied question, yes, when he thinks it over to himself – Why isn't going to an airport to observe what's going on more popular?. However, it works as a rhetorical question so it doesn't need an answer.

29   B

 Examiner Feedback

A: There is no evidence in the paragraph that he doesn't like doughnuts. He is just trying to get it at a lower price.

C: You can infer that this is wrong because he chooses to buy the doughnut. He must prefer the doughnut because the evidence is that he goes for the doughnut first.

30   He thinks it will give him some energy./He hopes that the sugar will give him energy.

 Examiner Feedback

Note that for this answer you have to use your inference skills and work out from the context what 'invigorating sugar-rush' means and how it will help him. You can see from his comment that he is 'still sleepy' so eating the doughnut doesn't appear to have worked. However, he takes up some activity. It's important in this answer therefore that you include the idea of 'hopes' or 'thinks'.

31   B

 Examiner Feedback

A: No, as the writer states that his expected sugary doughnut actually tastes of onion, so his hope of invigoration is dashed, not met.

C: Yes, the writer does describe the tunnels. But this distracts you from the real purpose of the paragraph, which is to decide that physical exercise is needed.

Remember that Text 4 is the most challenging text on the Reading paper, so it likely that your R4 skills are being tested (draw inferences, make deductions, and recognise implicit meaning). It is not likely therefore that locating a key word and writing down the information near it will be correct, as that is an R1 skill. Have a quick review of the four assessment objectives – R1, R2, R3, R4 – and note how R3 and R4 are tested more in Text 3 and Text 4.

32 C

 Examiner Feedback

Note that both A and B also contain accurate details, so they work as distractors. It is an understanding of the idiom that will get you the mark. There are many idioms in English that relate to children and childhood. Here are two examples that could also have worked in paragraph 9 for the writer to make his point:

- as easy as child's play
- like a child in a sweetshop.

33 A

 Examiner Feedback

Note that A is correct because it is the best answer. There are elements of B and C in the writer's account of his 24 hours. He does focus on his trip to the airport, but only in the opening two paragraphs. He also describes feeling bored in phrases like 'wandering around', 'the show ends', 'Hoping for an invigorating sugar-rush', and in needing the action of the trolley game. These elements work to distract you from the main purpose of the article, which can also be worded as:

- to write a travelogue of a typical day at London's Heathrow airport
- to observe human behaviour and aspects of life at a busy airport
- to try to find the positives of spending 24 hours at a busy airport.

My score for Text 4	
What I found difficult	
What I have learnt	
Six ways I can improve	• _____ • _____ • _____ • _____ • _____ • _____

Reflecting on progress made and reaching higher levels

In this unit, you have had guided practice at completing a full Reading paper with the aim of learning more about the skills you need to increase your performance in the examination. We have helped you strengthen your knowledge of what is required, we have recapped the key skills and assessment objectives, and you have applied these skills and knowledge to help you feel confident and ready for the Reading paper.

On page 3 we asked you to estimate your levels of skills that are important to doing well in the exam. The table is repeated below. Don't look back at your original levels just yet – fill out the table below. Then compare the two tables and note what has changed.

Key skills	I think I need to improve in this area	I'm already quite good at this
Identifying a range of the different types of texts and noting the differences between them		
Skimming to get a feel of what the text is about (the gist) and locating the key points and main ideas quickly		
Scanning for a closer look at a text to locate specific details		
Checking the verbs to identify the specific verb tenses and which tense a text as a whole is using		
Identifying the main purpose of a text		
Knowing and using language relating to themes and topics		
Being aware of language devices (tools) – the language skills a writer uses on purpose for effect and to create impact		
Using inference to work out what is meant from clues and hints		
Using deduction to work out what is meant by a logical analysis of the information that is given		

This is a reflective exercise and we want you to think about where you have improved.

- Do you feel that you have been able to recap on all of the main skills needed for the Reading paper?

- Are you feeling confident about the range of themes and topics that you might be reading about?

- Do you have a good understanding now of how the Reading paper is constructed and how the questions are set?

If the answers to those questions are positive, then you are well on the way to success.

⚙ Knowledge

What do I need to know about the Listening paper?

The recordings that you will be listening to will be from familiar scenarios, mostly relating to situations that people find themselves in, such as students at school and adults talking about general matters. One of the recordings might focus on a less familiar context with specific details and language – we will come to that later.

In the Listening paper, you will be engaging with all the themes and topics as set out in the specification.

Theme one – Identity and culture

Theme two – Local, national, international and global areas of interest

Theme three – Current and future study and employment

You need to know:

- the structure of the Listening paper, including how the recordings are played

- the themes and topics that occur, which will help you predict what to expect in the recordings

- the range of question types and how you are expected to write down your answers

- how you will be assessed by the examiners – in other words, where you will gain marks and how best to optimise this to raise your grade

- experience of how the speakers on the recordings use spoken English

You will help to develop your understanding by working through practice questions and reading the relevant features like those listed in the 'How to use this book' section on pages v–vi. The transcript is included at the end of each task for reference.

Here is a reminder of how the Listening paper works.

> - After the question number is announced, there will be a pause to allow you to read the instructions and questions.
>
> - Listen carefully to the recording and read the questions again.
>
> - Listen to the recording again and then answer the questions.
>
> - When the next question is about to start you will hear a bleep.
>
> - You may write at any time during the test.
>
> - Answer the questions in English.

Assessment Objectives: Listening

Understand and respond to spoken language

L1: Identify key details from a range of short and longer texts.

L2: Identify the overall message and key points in a variety of short and longer spoken texts, involving some more complex language.

L3: Understand and collate information from a variety of short and longer spoken texts, involving some complex language and more abstract material.

L4: Recognise purpose, implied meaning, attitudes and feelings in extended texts.

Recap

What are the key skills I will need for success in the Listening paper?

Let's recap the key listening skills using the specification and explore what they mean:

"Demonstrate general and specific understanding of different types of spoken language."

What does this mean for you?

There are two elements to this skill, and both are described further below. You also need to be aware of different types of spoken language. But what does this mean exactly?

In listening, we use the word 'scenario' and it will appear throughout this unit. A **scenario** can be defined as 'a setting in which a sequence of events takes place'. A range of scenarios feature across the five tasks in the Listening paper. Two examples of scenarios are: listening carefully to an announcement at a train station because your platform has been changed, and listening to a lecture at university on the condition of the railways in your country. Can you see how different types of listening skills are needed in these two scenarios?

- **Listening for gist** means listening to understand the context and be able to give a short summary of the main idea. You can use various ways to get the gist: establish the setting and background, ask yourself why the speakers are speaking, what their general aim is, and what the expected follow-up or response from the listener is.

- **Listening for specific details** involves engaging with the details of what the speakers are saying, and breaking down their spoken language into segments that contain the information you need. When a person is talking to you – as in a discussion – you can stop the person and ask them to repeat, explain, or add further details. If you are listening to a recording, you can pause it, take time to think, and then replay the recording. Of course, you cannot pause the recording during your exam!

In your Listening exam, you will need to listen for gist and also for specific details. These are basic listening skills, and the beginning of the exam will target these skills.

"Follow and understand clear standard speech using familiar language across a range of specified contexts."

What does this mean for you?

- **Standard English:** The recordings used in the Listening exam will be spoken by people whose first language is English and they will be speaking using Standard English. We can define Standard English as 'the form of English language that is widely accepted to be the usual, correct form'. As users of English as a Second Language, you will be learning Standard English at school – but you might not be using Standard English at home or with your friends.

- **Familiar language:** The actual spoken words in the exam scenarios have been selected to be familiar – that is, not technical, and you are likely to know most or many of them, and the exam is a test of listening skills more than a test of vocabulary. However, the more words you know, the better your chance of understanding what you hear.

"Identify the overall message, key points, details and opinions in a variety of short and longer spoken passages, involving some more complex language, recognising the relationship between past, present and future events."

What does this mean for you?

As the Listening exam progresses, the tasks become more challenging, the scenarios become longer and more detailed, and Tasks 4 and 5 are likely to use complex language. Let's look at this in more detail:

- **Key points:** In a longer scenario, you will hear speakers talk for quite a long time. Therefore, you need to listen carefully for the key points.

- **Opinions:** It's very difficult to engage in a longer discussion or a longer speech without giving an opinion! Sometimes it's easier to hear what a speaker's opinion is – for example, "I don't like it here." Sometimes you have to work harder to understand an opinion. For example, "Let's sit over there," could mean the same thing as the first example, but you have to work it out.

- **Complex language:** It is useful to listen to a variety of topics with a broad range of language. Listening to some adult source material – such as news reports and podcasts – will help stretch your vocabulary and increase your knowledge of idioms used in English.

- **Past, present, and future:** If a speaker is talking for longer, you will need to establish whether their focus is current or not. In most cases on the Listening paper, the tenses will be past and present. It is useful to revise your knowledge of common verbs and also try to listen to speakers using them to show past, present, or future actions. Qualifiers might be used (along with verbs in the past tense) such as 'yesterday', 'before', 'earlier', and 'previously', as well as phrases such as 'already done that' and 'taken care of it' – both of which refer to actions in the past.

"Deduce meaning from a variety of short and longer spoken texts, involving some complex language and more abstract material, including short narratives and authentic material addressing a wide range of contemporary and cultural themes."

What does this mean for you?

- **Abstract material:** Most of what you will hear on the recordings will be regular, straightforward announcements or conversations between people about everyday matters. However, the more challenging tasks might include abstract material. You can think of 'abstract' as meaning theoretical or talking about a concept. For example, if a scientist is talking about her vision of a virtual laboratory where she can do her experiments, this is an abstract idea. Try to imagine a visual picture in your mind – that way you can make the abstract idea or concept more meaningful to you.

- **Narratives:** In Task 5, for example, you might be listening to a talk given by someone about a particular subject or topic. Because the speaker is talking at length, the result is a narrative. Think of this as a sequence of connected events, or items, that all link to a common theme. It's not a narrative in terms of literature – to be clear, the Listening paper will not test you on literature, novels, or poems.

- **Authentic (material):** 'Authentic' means real. This means that the settings and spoken content in all of the tasks will reflect real-life situations, and the types of monologues and discussions that you hear every day.

- **Contemporary and cultural themes:** You will hear people talking about different parts of the world and different cultures. The material you hear will be contemporary – that is, talking about the present, and relevant to what is happening in the world currently. It's a good idea therefore to keep up with matters of global importance.

For longer spoken texts, you will be assessed on your ability to recognise purpose, implied meaning, **attitudes**, and **feelings**. Physical feelings are different from emotional feelings and attitudes. A speaker might say how they feel physically - for example, "I feel cold today. Yesterday in the sunshine, I felt much warmer." Emotional feelings and attitudes offer more than a description of a physical feeling. For example, "I don't like cold weather. I feel happier when it's warm. In my opinion, when it's sunny, people feel more outgoing." Being able to recognise a feeling, and when that might turn into an attitude is a higher level listening skill.

> *"Recognise and respond to key information, important themes and ideas in more extended spoken text, including authentic sources, adapted and abridged, as appropriate, by being able to answer questions, extract information, evaluate and draw conclusions."*

What does this mean for you?

You do not need not worry about adapted (changed) and abridged (shortened) sources – they just mean that what you hear could be based on longer and slightly different original recordings. The recordings you hear for each task will be standalone, which means you are not required to have listened to anything else. As far as you are concerned, what you hear for each task is complete.

Reflect

Reflecting on my current listening skills

Complete the table below right now with an estimate of your current skills. Just tick the box that you feel is closest to your level. That's all you need to do at the moment. We will return to this later.

Key skills	I think I need to improve in this area	I'm already quite good at this
Working out the overall meaning (the gist) of short statements		
Understanding the gist when more complex language is spoken		
Working out the overall message of longer talks when a single person is speaking		
Working out and organising the messages when more than one speaker is involved		
Listening for and locating specific details and information		
Understanding spoken Standard English		
Being familiar with the vocabulary – the words and phrases – used by speakers with different purposes		
Recognising when different tenses are used together – the relationship between past, present, and future events		
Recognising when a speaker gives an opinion		
Recognising when a speaker shows their feelings and attitudes in telling longer accounts		
In abstract scenarios and longer accounts, being able to infer what speakers are implying		

Apply

What is the best way for me to apply this knowledge and these skills to practise for the Listening paper?

Task 1

Let's start with Task 1, the first set of questions you will see in the Listening paper.

Common scenarios

Scenarios that have featured in previous exams include:

- where I would go if I won a lottery (first person)
- how to take a formal photograph of yourself (second person)
- ordering food and drinks (first person)
- posting a parcel at a posting office (first person)
- announcement in an airport to update passengers of a delay (third person)
- using electronic devices for different reasons (first person)
- planning for birthdays (first person)
- weather forecast (third person)
- news bulletin (third person)
- booking a holiday on the telephone (first person)
- studying to be a doctor (first person)
- summary of a schedule on a television channel (third person).

What do we notice about Task 1?

There will be one person speaking, with a clear purpose in mind, and it will be quite short. The wide-ranging scenarios in Task 1 are likely to include:

- a statement made by someone about themselves
- advice from another person
- an announcement in a range of situations
- a transaction that we carry out in regular daily life.

What are the key assessment elements of Task 1?

Marks available	Number of words	How I will gain marks
8 marks – 8 questions	30–50 words for each of the 4 recordings	• by identifying key details from a range of short and longer texts (L1)

Key Points

Task 1 is made up of four short statements and all the questions will be multiple choice. You will see that each question for Task 1 has quite short answers. This is because you are listening for specific details, and each suggested answer (A, B, and C) lists only details.

If you hear the detail quickly from the recording and you are confident it is correct, then you can record the answer. If you have any doubt, when you hear the recording a second time you can check your preferred answer – the one you think is most likely – and the other two suggested answers. It will not take much time, and you will probably be able to identify at least one answer that is wrong or not relevant. This is a good strategy to use for all of Task 1.

Assessment Objectives

L1. You will only be asked to identify key details and information. This means that you don't need to worry about the overall message, and you won't have to collate information from the different parts you hear.

Examiner Input

Even though you don't have much time in the Listening paper, you do have some reading time before the recording starts. For Task 1, these are probably the most important things to note:

- You are going to hear four short statements.
- There is no need to panic because you will hear them all twice.
- Each statement will have some specific details or information that you need to listen for.
- There will be a straightforward and single purpose to each statement, so you need to listen out for that.
- You have to answer multiple-choice questions only for Task 1. Look carefully at the three possible answers as it may help you to select the correct one as you hear the recording.

Language Support

In Task 1, the speaker might use the first, second, or third person. The statements are quite short and are usually only a few spoken sentences. Here's an example of how the same statement can be made using three different voices:

- "Oh dear. I needed to catch that 4.15pm train to Calcutta but the announcement said that engineering work means it's been cancelled. I'll have to take the 5.15pm train now."
- "If you are waiting for the 4.15pm train to Calcutta, please note that it has been cancelled due to engineering work. You should use the 5.15pm service instead."
- "The 4.15pm train is no longer running due to engineering work. The next available train will be the 5.15pm.

Exam-style questions

Now let's look at an example of Task 1 and the types of questions you are likely to be asked.

In the Listening paper, you will hear each recording twice. In this practice unit we advise you to play each recording once, take a look at the questions, then play the recording a second time. After this, you should answer the question before moving on to the next recording.

 Now listen carefully to the audio for **Task 1 Number 1** on the website. You can listen to each statement twice.

Write the correct letter in the box for questions **01.1** and **01.2**.

01.1 What does the speaker use to mix the butter with the flour?

A	Blender
B	Hands
C	Spoon

[1 mark]

01.2 How many millilitres of milk are needed in this recipe?

A	80
B	100
C	120

[1 mark]

Examiner Input

You are likely to get questions that start with 'How long …', 'How much …', 'How far …', 'What time …', and so on. For questions that ask you to identify a measure, listen carefully to the precise way in which the speaker states the measurement (for example, millilitres are not the same as litres).

 **Rephrasing**

Notice how the wording of the questions relating to the detail differs from the wording used by the speakers. For example, in an announcement in an airport about a flight bound for New Zealand, the question might ask where its destination is, because 'bound for' and 'destination' mean the same thing. In question 01.1, the word 'mix' is used, which means the same thing as 'combine' in the context. Learning **synonyms** (words with the same or a similar meaning) is an important skill you need to practise and refine, as it will feature a lot in the Listening paper.

Revision Tip

The Listening paper will test how accurately you have heard numbers, amounts, distances, times, and so on. You should practise listening to some that are close – for example, 'thirteen' and 'thirty'. Make sure you know the Standard English language measurements for:

- time (e.g. seconds, minutes, hours, weeks, months, years, decades)
- weights and measures (e.g. grams, kilograms/kilos, tonnes, millilitres, litres)
- distance (e.g. miles, kilometres). Note that miles are commonly used in the UK and in the USA, but you may also hear kilometres as these are a global measure of distance.

Be prepared for any of the common measurements to be tested and make sure you have learnt how these are written down. This is called notation. For example, kilograms are kg, millilitres are ml, and hours can be written as hrs. Millions are written as m and billions as bn, so 4 million = 4m and 4 billion = 4 bn. Try to learn as many as you can, but not as if you are studying a science subject!

Now listen to **Task 1 Number 2**. Write the correct letter in the box for questions **02.1** and **02.2**.

02.1 What is useful about the lifejacket?

A	It is operated by a cord.
B	It is very up to date.
C	It is heavy in the water.

[ ]

[1 mark]

02.2 What can you use a torch for?

A	To seek help
B	To see in the dark
C	To see the crew

[ ]

[1 mark]

(!) Exam Tip

Be careful not to just listen for key words and then choose your answer because it contains that word. For example, Answer A includes the word 'cord'. However, by listening carefully we can establish that the lifejacket does not need a cord.

(!) Exam Tip

Don't forget that you are not tested on prior knowledge of a subject – the same as in the Reading paper. For example, in question 02.2, you will know that a torch shines a light and is commonly used when it's dark. But you need to ask, is that the specific detail about the torch that has been mentioned?

(Q) Examiner Input

In a similar way to the Reading paper, try to spot the key words in a question, such as 'what', 'who', 'why', 'where', 'when', and so on. There will be time to look at each question carefully, and you might find it helpful to do this whilst you listen to the recording for the first time. Sometimes, time spent analysing a question can point to a likely answer. Remember, examiners use distractors and other answers that appear possible at first glance.

Now listen to **Task 1 Number 3**. Write the correct letter in the box for questions **03.1** and **03.2**.

03.1   When will the first speaker start talking?

A	9am
B	10am
C	11am

[   ]

[1 mark]

03.2   What will her colleague focus on at the meeting?

A	Traffic levels on roads
B	Falling pollution in polar regions
C	Effect of more air travel

[   ]

[1 mark]

Now listen to **Task 1 Number 4**. Write the correct letter in the box for questions **04.1** and **04.2**.

04.1   What is grown in the garden centre?

A	Fruit and flowers
B	Fruit and vegetables
C	Vegetables and juice

[   ]

[1 mark]

04.2   What was the speaker **not** expecting in her new job?

A	To be tired when working
B	To be working with vegetables
C	To be cold when working

[   ]

[1 mark]

(!) **Exam Tip**

The context is a meeting about global warming and pollution – so be careful not to rely too much on your prior knowledge about this issue. You have probably studied the topic in other classes, and you may know a range of vocabulary and phrases associated with it, such as melting ice caps, climate change, emissions, pollution, congested traffic, carbon footprint, and so on. However, remember that you are being tested on your listening skills and it's the recording's specific words that you need to recognise – be careful not to use the vocabulary you have learnt before because those words might not have the same meaning as the words used by the speaker – that is, they might not be synonymous.

(!) **Exam Tip**

You might be asked to consider more than one item in an answer. If so, the order of the items might not be the same in the suggested answers as were spoken – so look out for this. Also, be clear about how many items are required. Lists are usually of similar items. Lists that have appeared in previous exams are coats, hats, scarves (cold weather clothing), and news, report, tennis, film (television schedule).

! Exam Tip

Notice how the suggested answers for question 04.2 all have a similar appearance. Each answer has five words and starts with 'To be'. This is a common technique in multiple-choice answers – to make them look similar. You can expect this in your Listening paper, and it's good to be aware of expected formats. Whilst the Listening paper is obviously a test of your listening skills, you will also need to be very careful when reading. Look at the answers for question 04.2 – they may follow the same format, but are all very different.

Revision Tip

Listen carefully for words that sound similar or the same. Of course, you will be trying to listen hard in the examination during the 40 minutes. If two words sound similar – for example 'produce' and 'juice', listen for the number of syllables, and consonant and vowel sounds. Try to practise similar sounding words in your revision, noting the difference in pronunciation and meaning.

Revision Tip

There is evidence that people need to understand the purpose whilst listening to someone before they can engage fully. Sometimes, we have to stop a person whilst they are speaking and ask them to clarify: "What do you mean?" We need to get the gist, or the 'bigger picture', so that we can process our understanding and response. In the Listening paper, the same applies to you. Whenever someone talks to you, try to establish the purpose as soon as you can. This is called *listening for* rather than *listening to*. This will help develop your pre-listening skills, and you can start to do this as soon as you see a question on the paper. Ask yourself: What am I expecting the speaker(s) to talk about? What is their purpose for talking? For Task 1, we could describe the speakers' purposes as:

- to show an audience how to make a recipe
- to carry out a safety check on a boat
- to introduce the first two speakers at a meeting
- to say something about the first few weeks in a new job.

Examiner feedback and raising my grade

How well did you do on Task 1? There are 8 marks available. Check your answers with the correct answers below. Note the feedback from the examiner to help you understand why a particular answer is correct and why some alternative answers are not correct.

Examiner Input

In Task 1, examiners will only be marking your answers to eight multiple-choice questions (MCQs). Try not to predict any patterns, for example A, B, C, A, B, C, A, B. This is not how the questions are set. However, it is unlikely that all of the answers will be Answer A. If your answers are all Bs, for example, it would be a good idea to review your answers. It's more likely that some As, some Bs, and some Cs will feature. It's highly likely that in a series of eight MCQs all three possible answers will feature at least once.

Answers to Task 1

Questions 01–04

01.1 B

(Q) Examiner Feedback

A chef or a cook could use a blender (Answer A) or a spoon (Answer C) to make the recipe, but the speaker prefers to use his hands. A and C are therefore distractors as spoon and blend (as a verb) are mentioned.

01.2 C

(Q) Examiner Feedback

Answers A and B are wrong, as they state 80 and 120. This is an example of when precise listening skills are important.

02.1 B

(Q) Examiner Feedback

Answer A is wrong. Listening carefully, we can hear that you *don't* need to pull a cord with this lifejacket. Answer C states that the lifejacket is heavy when it is in the water, but we know this is not useful as we are told that it is lightweight.

02.2 A

(Q) Examiner Feedback

At the very end, the speaker mentions the torch twice. Yes, the torch can be used if help is needed or, put another way, 'to seek help' (probably by holding it up and waving it sideways). It is true that we use torches to see in the dark (Answer B), but this is not why a torch is provided as a safety measure – it's to show anyone who is nearby, perhaps on another boat, at night that help is needed. There is no evidence for Answer C, even though it's possible that the people on a boat might use a torch to see each other at night.

03.1 B

👤 Examiner Feedback

Be sure to know your times and the various ways in English they are reported. For example, the 24-hour clock may also be used, which would put 10am at 10.00 and 10pm at 22.00. Answer A is wrong as it's coffee time and not the proper meeting yet. Answer C is a distractor, because at 11am the second speaker at the conference delivers their talk.

03.2 C

👤 Examiner Feedback

Answer A might seem reasonable, as we know from prior knowledge that cars and trucks on roads are a major global polluter, but listen carefully because it's 'air' traffic that is the focus. Answer B is an example where a relevant word ('pollution') appears in the recording, but the word before it (falling) changes the idea completely.

04.1 B

👤 Examiner Feedback

Answer A mentions flowers. This is not mentioned by the speaker. Although flowers are likely to be also grown where she works, be careful not to infer too much. Answer C includes 'juice' which sounds like 'produce' but is not the same thing. It tries to distract you.

04.2 C

👤 Examiner Feedback

In the recording, the speaker says she is colder than she thought she would be, so Answer C sums this up but uses different words. Answer A may well be true, as it is a new job, but there is no evidence of this in what has been said. In Task 1, you are not expected to infer, so if the detail is not there it cannot be a correct answer. Answer B is a close attempt, but the speaker only says it's great to be working with vegetables – at no point does she say she was either expecting or not expecting this. Remember that questions can be set using negatives.

My score for Task 1	
What I found difficult	
What I have learnt	
Two ways I can improve	• •

Transcript

Task 1

M1 Let me tell you how I make this. First, I combine the flour and butter using my hands. Some chefs will add yoghurt with a spoon, but not me. I add 120 millilitres of milk. Once the mixture blends together, we can add the fruit.

F1 About using safety measures. Your lifejacket uses brand new technology and you don't need to pull a cord. It is also lightweight. We've given you a small first-aid kit and a torch. The torch you can use to shine a light so someone might see you.

F2 Okay everybody, after coffee at 9, the meeting will begin properly this morning at 10 when our speaker will update us on how fast the ice caps are melting in the polar regions. At 11am, her colleague will link this to rising pollution caused by increased air travel.

F3 I started my part-time job three weeks ago. I'm very pleased as it's connected to my college studies. I'm learning about garden produce, so working in a place which grows vegetables and fruit is great. I didn't think it would be as cold and dirty as it is.

Task 2

Now let's look at Task 2, and how it is structured in the Listening paper.

Common scenarios

Settings and scenarios that have featured in previous exams include:

- A student is seeking advice about his parents' decision to move house, and he is concerned about how to keep in touch with his friends and make new friends. The adviser suggests he joins clubs, plays sports, and takes up new hobbies.

- A person is asked about watching films – the genre he prefers and the ways in which he watches them. He goes to the cinema, but likes also to watch at home on a laptop to save money.

- A woman who has recently moved into an area goes to a hairdresser and is told about the range of local facilities, such as shops and restaurants. She also finds out about a charity hike (a long walk) at the weekend, and the annual art festival.

- An International GCSE student is discussing subject choices for A level with his careers tutor, who advises him to think about what happens after A levels. The student considers journalism, but is also unsure of whether he wants to go to university.

- Two women discuss how to reduce the amount of plastic that is produced unnecessarily, by changing their habits and reusing and recycling – and by seeking out food stalls that don't use plastic boxes.

What do we notice about Task 2?

Task 2 is a dialogue between, for example, two students discussing their lives, their school, or university, or between two adults discussing a topical issue. The scenario is likely to be semi-formal. The topics vary, so you can expect a wide range – but a common theme is everyday life, so there will not be anything too technical.

What are the key assessment elements of Task 2?

Marks available	Number of words	How I will gain marks
8 marks – usually 4 questions, sometimes 5	broken into segments of 30–50 words – usually 4–6 segments	• by identifying the overall message and key points in a variety of short and longer spoken texts, involving some more complex language (L2) • by understanding and collating information, from a variety of short and longer spoken texts, involving some complex language and more abstract material (L3)

Key Points

The questions for Task 2 are not multiple-choice questions. Instead, you will respond to open questions by writing on the answer lines provided in the examination paper. Try not to complicate things by using too many of your own words as this might result in unclear meaning. The best approach is to use as few words as possible, and you can use words from the recording. Task 2 usually asks you to look for linked information where two details have been talked about.

Assessment Objectives

L2 and L3. This task is more challenging than Task 1, and it focuses on working out what the overall message is, and the key points that support this. You will also need to collate information from parts of the text.

Exam-style questions

Now let's look at an example of Task 2 and the types of questions you are likely to be asked.

Alan is applying to join a local gym. He is discussing his application with the receptionist.

Pre-listening

You know from the description under the task who the speakers are and what the context is. So, what are the most important things to note?

- It's a conversation between a man who wants to join a gym and someone from the gym who is helping him with his application.

- Think quickly about what you know already about gyms and membership of gyms.

- What useful vocabulary do you know relating to the types of exercise that people do in gyms? It might well help your understanding, but remember that you are being tested on your listening skills and it's the recording's specific words that you need to recognise and use in your answers.

- The purpose seems to be clear. Alan wants to join and the staff member is helping him. But what information might Alan be asked to provide?

Revision Tip

Anticipating what might be spoken, in semi-formal dialogues is a really useful skill. Build up your knowledge of these types of settings and the linked vocabulary – for example gyms, health centres, libraries, offices, careers centres, and so on – in your revision. Hopefully, you will already have some awareness of the settings and the types of conversations that happen in them.

Examiner Input

The Listening paper is not an examination of your writing skills. This means that do you not need to worry about fully accurate spelling, for example. Close attempts at words will be accepted by examiners as long as they can recognise the word by reading it out loud. For example, if an answer is 'medical' but you wrote 'medicalle', 'meddikall', or 'medicle' this would be fine. If you don't know how to spell a word you have heard, focus on the number of syllable sounds (medical has three) and try to spell using this approach – med-i-cal.

 Now listen to the audio for **Task 2** on the website. You can listen to each statement twice.

Listen carefully to the discussion and answer questions **05** to **08**.

05 Alan needs to give more details to the receptionist.

List **two** things Alan confirms. [2 marks]

1 _____

2 _____

06 List **two** health issues Alan mentions. [2 marks]

1 _____

2 _____

07 Alan mentions reasons why he wants to join a gym.

List **two** reasons which are not related to his health. [2 marks]

1 _____

2 _____

08 According to the staff member how can lunchtime sessions assist Alan?

List **two** advantages. [2 marks]

1 _____

2 _____

! Exam Tip

Don't have too many attempts at an answer. In other words, where there are two items required and two lines provided, only write two items/things. If you add more, an examiner will not look at the extra items. So 'list two examples' means only two – not three, in a hope that the two correct examples will be there. You don't want the correct one to be your third example, and then lose the mark because your second answer is wrong.

Remember also to provide sufficient details – you gain nothing by only writing one detail where two are requested.

Each question will specify how many marks it is worth and how many details are needed, so these rules apply across all parts of the Listening paper.

! Exam Tip

Be careful not to change the meaning of what a speaker says. In Task 2, you are challenged to show that you have understood an overall message. Alan wants to join a gym for health reasons but also for other reasons. He wants a change. However, his change is quite specific, so if you wrote down 'change his life' that would not be the same meaning as it suggests a much bigger issue. All he says is that he sits down a lot at work, not that he is unhappy with his job or his life in general.

◉ Examiner Input

Remember to always be listening for rather than listening to. This will help you develop your pre-listening skills. Ask yourself: What am I expecting the speaker(s) to talk about? What is their purpose for talking? For Task 2, we would describe the speakers' purposes as follows:

The staff member at the gym is speaking so that she can:

- obtain further details from Alan, who wants to join
- provide details about the lunchtime sessions in order to meet Alan's needs.

Alan is speaking so that he can:

- inform the gym that he has some minor medical issues
- add some reasons why he wants to join the lunchtime sessions.

Examiner feedback and raising my grade

How well did you do on Task 2? There are 8 marks available. Check your answers with the correct answers below. Note the feedback from the examiner to help you understand why a particular answer is correct and why some alternative answers are not correct.

Examiner Input

In Task 2, examiners will give you credit for answers that show you have understood the overall message and that you have been able to collate details from parts of the recording. They will read carefully the short answers you have provided and if the meaning is clear, despite any spelling errors, you will get the mark(s).

Answers to Task 2

Questions 05–08

> 05 Any two of the following:
> - (He) works full-time
> - (He) works in an office
> - (His) medical issues
> - (His) postcode

Examiner Feedback

Remember, where you see brackets ( ) on a mark scheme (such as *he* and *his* in the answer above), it means that you can give that information but you don't need it to get the mark(s). Writing fuller details takes more time, so it's good to practise writing down just what is needed.

Other sample answers that would be accepted for question 05:

✓ Alan has a full-time job./His office work is full-time. He is employed full-time.

✓ his medical condition/what his medical problem is/medical needs

Answers that an examiner would not accept, and the reasons why:

✗ the online form – No, this is how he provided the details, not what they are.

✗ Alan/he works for a time (in an office) – This would mean that you misheard 'full-time' as 'for a time', and would therefore be wrong as it is not the same idea.

✗ he has an issue – No, the key point is that it is a medical issue.

✗ his doctor's details – No, this would be adding details that are not spoken about in the recording.

✗ a bit more information – No, this is the first part only and lacks an understanding of the question and what the staff member needs.

> 06   Any two of the following:
>
> - (Slightly) overweight
> - High heart rate/Raised heart rate (or heartbeat)
> - Allergic to eggs

Examiner Feedback

Other sample answers that would be accepted for question 06:

✓ has a problem with his heart going too fast/pulse rate is (slightly) high

✓ He feels that he is too heavy./His weight is too much.

✓ Eggs make him very ill.

Answer that an examiner would not accept, and why:

✗ He has an allergy – This is not enough, as the key point is that he is allergic to eggs. Note that 'allergy' or 'allergic' could be spelled in a variety of ways and be accepted (for example, alurgy, hallergey, alargie) – but now that you have seen the word, remember it!

> 07   Reasons Alan mentions:
>
> - Get out of the office
> - Break his (lunch) routine (that he has got into)

Examiner Feedback

Other sample answers that would be accepted for question 07:

✓ get away from (his) workplace/take a break from the office

✓ change his (lunch) routine/break the pattern he has got used to (for lunch).

Answers that an examiner would not accept, and why:

✗ He is tired of his work – No, because this is a different idea. There is no evidence Alan is tired of or does not enjoy his work. It's just that he needs to energise himself at lunchtime. Be careful of an answer that changes the meaning to something else.

✗ eat a healthier lunch – No, this is a distractor because it's not Alan who says this. It's a general remark by the member of staff.

08   Advantages of lunchtime sessions:
- Can help with (Alan's) social life
- (Helps) people eat healthier lunches/meals

Examiner Feedback

Other sample answers that would be accepted for question 08:

✓ can help Alan meet people/improve social life

✓ People eat healthier food./(helps) people choose healthier options/
   food choices.

Answers that an examiner would not accept, and why:

✗ They are busy – No, as this can be taken two ways. Busy means
   more than popular – and it can be a negative thing, a disadvantage.
   This is where an answer changes the original meaning and blurs
   the original meaning.

✗ will help with a special life – No, this would mean you have
   misheard social for special.

✗ People eat smaller meals – No, because whilst this might be what
   some people do, healthier does not necessarily mean smaller.
   There is no evidence in the recording that the staff member
   thinks this.

My score for Task 2	
What I found difficult	
What I have learnt	
Three ways I can improve	• _____ • _____ • _____

Transcript

Task 2

F1 Hi Alan. Thanks for the details you provided on our online form. Just a couple of things to clear up please. You work full-time in an office don't you so I'll add that. Can I have more information about the medical issues you mentioned? Oh, and also your postcode.

M1 I wanted to tell you in person that I feel I am slightly overweight. My other condition is that I have a high heart rate that I was born with. I don't take medicine for it, but as this is a gym, I'd better mention it. Oh, I'm also allergic to eggs.

F1 Okay, thanks for explaining. I'm guessing then that you've decided to join our gym to improve your general health and to shed a little weight?

M1 Yes, for those reasons, but also hopefully to get out of the office. I am sitting down most of the time at work, and I eat lunch at my desk. I'm hoping that these lunchtime sessions in the gym will break the routine I've got into.

F1 Sounds perfect. And we have many members like you, who come to exercise from 12pm to about 1.30pm. Our lunchtime sessions are very popular. Might help with your social life too. Many people also say it helps them to eat healthier lunches.

Task 3

Now let's look at Task 3, and how it is structured in the Listening paper.

Common scenarios

Settings and scenarios that have featured in previous exams include:

- A spokesperson talks about a newly opened gym, which is looking to attract new members and is offering membership deals.

- A woman talks about her mother's life as a Turkish immigrant to the UK and how she worked hard through a difficult early life to later train to be a doctor.

- A chef explains how he is going to cook a stir fry using vegetables he has grown in his own garden. He also talks about how home-grown is better and how it's important for children to eat their greens (vegetables).

- In her podcast, a woman describes a visit to see her brother, who lives on another continent. She talks about the quality time spent and also about her sister who lives locally. She compares and contrasts these family relationships.

- A professional photographer talks about his specialism of photographing wild animals and recalls some anecdotes of interesting and unusual locations. He approves of cameras in mobile phones as a great addition to his craft.

What do we notice about Task 3?

Task 3 is a monologue – that is, only one person is speaking. For example, the person might be:

- recalling moments in their lives and places they have been (autobiographical)

- talking about what they do as a career (such as cooking, photography, gym manager).

Autobiographical anecdotes on interesting and unusual moments might feature.

What are the key assessment elements of Task 3?

Marks available	Number of words	How I will gain marks
8 marks – usually 4 questions, including 1 question that is worth 3 marks	broken into segments of 40–80 words – usually 4 segments	• by understanding and collating information from a variety of short and longer spoken texts, involving some complex language and more abstract material (L3)

Key Points

The answer sheet in the exam is set up for you as a series of notes, with subheadings. It's likely that there will be four subheadings and each one will require you to write in single-word answers, to complete the notes. The notes are full sentences, so you can check that your inserted word creates the meaning you intend and makes a proper sentence.

There are rules about what examiners will accept and we will look at these, but take note that synonyms are not accepted. You are being assessed on your listening skill – and in this task it's a case of writing down the exact word you have heard from the recording that you think fits best.

Assessment Objectives

L3. This task focuses on only one assessment objective. All the questions test your skill in collecting, combining, and organising information to show your understanding.

Exam-style questions

Now let's look at an example of Task 3 and the types of questions you are likely to be asked.

> Fo is talking on her podcast about a vegetarian festival she visited in China.

Pre-listening

You know from the description under the task who the speaker is and what the specific context is. So, what are the most important things to note?

- It's a talk given by one person and it focuses on a vegetarian festival the speaker was at in China.

- Think whether you know anything about Chinese festivals. Remember not to panic if you don't, because all of the details you are tested on will come from what you hear. Your previous knowledge is not being tested.

- What about vegetarianism? Perhaps you know something about that. If so, you could listen out for the parts that discuss not eating meat.

- Do you know any useful vocabulary relating to festivals? This is travel writing – or rather, speaking about a travel experience – so you can probably expect some travel words and phrases. However, be careful not to use your own vocabulary about festivals in your answers because it might have a different meaning to that in the recording.

- Ask yourself: Is there a hidden message coming? Is this just about a vegetarian festival in China or is there more to it? Will its purpose be to try to convince others to take up a non-meat diet?

Revision Tip

Anticipating what will be spoken in monologues such as this, which are international and based on a travel and tourism, is a useful skill as you might hear more recordings like this. Having some prior knowledge of global destinations is useful for this examination.

Now listen to the audio for **Task 3** on the website. You can listen to the recording twice.

Listen carefully to the discussion and answer questions **09** to **12**.

09 Podcast – *Fo's Festivals*:

The festival in China is annual, lasts a fortnight and it is

_____ for all. **[1 mark]**

10 History:

Some miners had been digging to find _____

and became sick. After eating a vegetable-based diet the miners

_____ and it's this that is still

celebrated. **[2 marks]**

11 Not allowed:

During the festival fortnight, people should not eat

_____ or _____

as they have a strong smell. An aim of the festival is to

give the body and mind a cleansing, and dressing in

_____ clothing is not allowed. **[3 marks]**

12 After the festival:

Street food vendors start selling _____

dishes again and this can be a problem.

Fo thinks that people should have a _____

about what they eat. **[2 marks]**

(!) Exam Tip

For Task 3, only one word is required in each space. As a general rule, where more than one answer is provided examiners will only mark your first attempt. If you include an extra attempt, it will be ignored.

(!) Exam Tip

Do not try to use synonyms to fill in the gaps for Task 3. These are not accepted, as the objective is to locate and collate the correct detail that was spoken. In this task, that is an exact word. So, although you might think an exact synonym is correct – and it may well be – that is not what you are being asked to do in this part of the exam.

Language Support

Where an answer requires a verb, the use of the correct verb tense is important in Task 3. Getting the tense wrong can cause your answer to become uncertain. You may still get the marks if you use a different tense, but it is risky, so try to stay in the same tense as in the recording.

Examiner Input

Spelling: If you don't feel fully confident about spelling a word, stay with the same number of syllables that you have heard and examiners will try to reward you if your attempt is close. One thing to bear in mind is that if your spelling attempt creates another word that is common in English, the examiner will probably not be allowed to award a mark as the whole meaning will be changed. Homophones – words that sound the same but are spelled differently – are therefore not normally accepted. For example, if the word you are listening for is 'meat' but you spell this as 'meet' you will not get the mark.

Grammar: Remember that you are not being assessed for grammatical accuracy in the Listening exam. Grammatical accuracy is assessed in the Writing paper and speaking correctly is assessed in the Speaking test. However, be careful not to use phrases that cause confusion as a result of poor grammar, as this could lose you marks. It's probably best to keep your grammar simple in answering questions in all of the five tasks on the Listening paper.

Revision Tip

When you hear something, your brain sometimes creates a visual image of what it hears. This means that listening is actually also a visual thing, and you can take advantage of this to help you understand and process what you are hearing. You could build on your mental image of what is being talked about by imagining that you are there at the scene. This could work well in scenarios where two people are in conversation, and you are listening in, or where there is a longer talk and you are 'in the audience', perhaps wanting to ask a question. Try to revise your familiarity with typical scenarios by imagining you are close to the action and try to avoid feeling that you are just a distant observer.

Examiner feedback and raising my grade

How well did you do on Task 3? There are 8 marks available. Check your answers with the correct answers below. Note the feedback from the examiner to help you understand why a particular answer is correct and why some alternative answers are not correct.

Examiner Input

In Task 3, examiners will give credit for answers that show you have been able to collate specific words from parts of the recording. They will check the words you have provided and as long as the meaning is clear you will get the mark(s). Remember, it's single words that you need to write down. If you have heard two words that you think are your answer, then choose the one that you think makes the meaning clear. For example, if you heard 'green door' then it will probably be 'door' that is required.

Examiner Input

You will not usually see any use of brackets, ( ), or a forward slash, /, on the mark scheme for Task 3, because only the key words spoken in the recording will be rewarded a mark. There are no alternative answers.

Answers to Task 3

Questions 09–12

09	free

Examiner Feedback

Other sample answers that would be accepted for question 09:

✓ fre – Yes, even though the spelling is wrong the meaning is clear, and 'fre' is not another word in the English language.

An answer that an examiner would not accept, and why:

✗ centred – No, because this changes the meaning of the use of 'centred' in the talk. Fo means that the festival has a large presence in the town. Also 'centred for all' doesn't have clear meaning.

10   copper
      recovered

Examiner Feedback

Other sample answers that would be accepted for question 10:

✓ coppa – Yes, because despite the spelling, the word 'coppa' sounds similar and has two syllables.

✓ recovery – Yes, if you use the noun (recovery) then the main idea is not changed.

Answers that an examiner would not accept, and why:

✗ cop her – No, because even though this sounds similar, there are two words. Remember, in Task 3, only one word is required. The examiner will look at the first word, 'cop', and not allow a mark. The two words used together, 'cop her', actually have a different meaning in English.

✗ got better – No, as Task 3 is testing your skill in listening for a single word. 'Got better' is a synonym for recovered, but synonyms are not rewarded in Task 3. Remember that only Assessment Objective L3 (Understand and collate information from a variety of short and longer spoken texts, involving some complex language and more abstract material) is being tested – your skill in collating details and presenting them as they are in the spoken text.

11   onions
      garlic
      colourful

Examiner Feedback

Other sample answers that would be accepted for question 11:

✓ onion – Yes, as the singular has the same idea and meaning as the plural.

✓ gahlik – Yes, as garlic is a tricky word to spell, and 'gahlik' sounds the same and does not make another word in English.

✓ coloured – Yes, as the meaning of 'coloured' is close enough in the context of clothing. Writing 'coloured' does not change the original word's meaning, and both words are adjectives so you have not changed the word class.

Examiner Feedback

Answers that an examiner would not accept for question 11, and why:

✗ pungent – No in either of the first two spaces, as the meaning of 'eat pungent' is unclear because it is missing a word. 'Eat pungent food' is the correct English. Also pungent means to have a strong smell, so putting pungent is repeating the same idea twice.

✗ disallowed – No, and for the same reason as above, because if you put this there would be a missing word (a word telling us what is disallowed).

✗ white – No, as you have picked up on the wrong idea. White clothing is permitted (not banned) at the festival.

| 12 | meat |
| | choice |

Examiner Feedback

Other sample answers that would be accepted for question 12:

✓ meate – Yes, as this spelling can be pronounced the same as meat, and 'meate' is not a word in English. However, as stated earlier, if you put 'meet' that would not be allowed.

✓ choyce – Yes, as this is very close despite its incorrect spelling.

Answers that an examiner would not accept, and why:

✗ cooking meat – No, because the first word will be the one that the examiner looks at and marks. 'Vendors start selling cooking meat dishes' doesn't make sense.

✗ vegetarian – No, as this doesn't make sense: 'people should have a vegetarian about what they eat'. Fo is clear in her view. People should have a choice, but – as she says – they can continue to eat good vegetarian food after the festival is over.

My score for Task 3	
What I found difficult	
What I have learnt	
Four ways I can improve	• _____ • _____ • _____ • _____

F1 Welcome to this week's edition of *Fo's Festivals* and I am going to tell you about the free vegetarian festival I have just been to in China. It happens annually and lasts a fortnight. It's centred around a town in the south, but over the last 40 years it has spread widely across the country and to other places like Singapore and Malaysia.

F1 The history is interesting. About 200 hundred years ago, in a community of miners who were digging for copper, many of the miners became ill but local people couldn't work out why. When they were not well, they ate a diet based on vegetables, and within a few weeks, the miners recovered. Nobody knows if eating meat caused any problems, but the recovery with their vegetarian diet is what was remembered and celebrated now.

F1 It's a strange thing, but some vegetables are not allowed during the vegetarian festival! For example, onions or garlic, as apparently these are just too pungent and one of the aims of the fortnight is to cleanse your body. Many people choose to wear white clothing and to use the festival as a sort of cleansing of the body and mind. The wearing of colourful clothes is banned.

F1 Some people criticise the festival because it only promotes vegetarianism for a short while. After the two weeks are up, it's back to normal and street food sales are focused again on meat cooked in saturated fats. We all know how bad this can be for some people, causing obesity and heart disease. But my view is that regarding food, people should always have a choice. There are plenty of restaurants in China that serve excellent vegetarian dishes all year round.

Task 4

Now let's look at Task 4, and how it is structured in the Listening paper.

Common scenarios

Settings and scenarios that have appeared in previous exams include:

- an interview with a college admissions officer to get advice for students who are in the process of applying for places and subjects to study

- an interview with an athlete – a long-distance runner – who talks about the challenges of getting older and still competing in races all over the world

- someone receiving advice from a friend about how to get a local part-time job to fund a gap year – she is advised to use an app and social media to get notifications of available work

- two male friends discussing the very different holidays they have just been on – one enjoyed a luxury, poolside, relaxing break and the other went camping, climbing, hiking, and canoeing

- a student discussing with her course leader how and where she can put on a festival to celebrate the end of studies for her class – with food stalls, local bands, and a film.

What do we notice about Task 4?

Task 4 is a dialogue, but the setting can vary from a radio interview to a private meeting, or to two friends having a discussion. You can also expect the following:

- a degree of formality – in other words, these are not people discussing casual matters as friends might, but discussing a topic that is more formal such as entry to college, professional running, part-time employment, types of holidays, and staging an event

- specific details will be included, perhaps specific advice from either one or both of the speakers. It is likely that both people are likely to contribute something to the discussion.

- it will be longer than Task 2, with more information provided

- adults or students might feature in Task 4 – or a combination of the two.

What are the key assessment elements of Task 4?

Marks available	Number of words	How I will gain marks
8 marks – usually 4 or 5 questions, including one question worth 3 marks that requires a list of 3 items	broken into segments of 50–100 words – speaker is likely to speak 2 or 3 times	<ul><li>by identifying key details from a range of short and longer texts (L1)</li><li>by understanding and collating information from information from a variety of short and longer spoken texts, involving some complex language and more abstract material (L3)</li></ul>

Key Points

There will be a combination of open questions and collation activities for you to complete for Task 4. You will be asked to answer questions directly and you can use your own words to add to the details you hear in the recording. It's also fine to just write down the short phrase, or even single word.

Assessment objective L1 is tested again in Task 4, so don't overcomplicate things, feeling that you have to explain with more detail than is actually needed. When making lists, it's best to keep the notes short, and for this reason, you will only be provided with one dotted line, so be sure to stay within the space. You won't need to write more, even if being asked to list items, examples, details, things, and so on.

 Assessment Objectives

L1 and L3. This task focuses on combining these two assessment objectives by listening to two people in a discussion. The questions test your skills in locating specific details, but also in collecting, combining, and organising information to show your understanding.

Exam-style questions

Now let's look at an example of Task 4 and the types of questions you are likely to be asked.

> Farida is being interviewed on a radio show called *Technology Update*. Farida discusses her work and college experience with drones.

 Pre-listening

You know from the description under the task who the two speakers are and what the context is – it's a radio interview. You can already establish that it's more formal. So, what are the most important things to note?

- It's a formal interview, so there will be planned questions that are likely to have been expected.
- Farida will talk mostly – or only – about drones, so you can plan ahead by reminding yourself what you know about drones and different ways they are used.
- Remind yourself of any technical vocabulary or jargon you know that relates to this type of electronics but remember to use the recording's vocabulary in your answers.
- Farida is working for a company, so she must have hands-on experience with drones.
- She also has college experience of studying drones, which must be quite technical.

Revision Tip

Anticipating what will be spoken in a more formal setting such as an interview on the radio or internet website is good practice for this examination. Technology is a popular topic, and very contemporary.

Examiner Input

Remember, you only have 5 minutes preparation time before you hear the recordings, so think only briefly about what you already know about the topic – prior knowledge will help you get a good sense of what is being said or discussed, but do not rely on it. Make sure you allow enough time to read the questions carefully.

Examiner Input

For Task 4 you **can** use synonyms and synonym phrases but you are strongly advised to locate the specific detail required and/or collate specific details if a list is required. If you do add some of your own words that work as synonyms, the examiner will award you the mark(s) if they have exactly the same meaning as the original.

Now listen to the audio for **Task 4** on the website. You can listen to the recording twice.

Listen carefully to the interview and answer questions **13** to **16**.

13   For how long has Farida been an apprentice?   **[1 mark]**

_____

_____

14   How often is Farida at her new college?   **[1 mark]**

_____

_____

15   What did Farida do with drones when she was younger?
List **three** things.   **[3 marks]**

1   _____

2   _____

3   _____

16.1   The interviewer says that the radio station uses drones.
Give **two** uses.   **[2 marks]**

1   _____

2   _____

16.2   Who is Farida currently making a drone for?   **[1 mark]**

_____

_____

Revision Tip

Even though time is limited in the Listening exam, you will still need to 'tune in' to the recording to focus on and understand the context. Practice will help you to do this quickly. You can revise this by thinking about the people talking and using these prompts:

- Who is speaking and what do you already know about them?
- Identify the topic quickly – what sort of ideas are you *expecting* to hear based on the topic and extending it?
- What do you want to find out about the speaker and the topic? This will help you engage actively with the speaker(s).
- Does the speaker ask any questions? Do they use rhetorical questions?
- Do you have any questions for the speaker?

Try 'tuning in' to some recordings you already have, and some new ones you can find. Use the five criteria above. Don't spend too long on this revision exercise, and don't make long notes. It's just about training your ears and brain to become more 'listening aware'.

Examiner feedback and raising my grade

How well did you do on Task 4? There are 8 marks available. Check your answers with the correct answers below. Note the feedback from the examiner to help you understand why a particular answer is correct and why some alternative answers are not correct.

 Examiner Input

In Task 4, examiners will try to give you credit for answers that show you have been able to listen for, locate, and provide the correct details. They will check the words you have given and as long as the meaning is clear, despite any spelling and grammar errors, you will get the mark(s).

 Examiner Input

In Task 4, you are looking for specific information and details. You don't need to use your own words to answer the questions – you can 'lift' the words and phrases from the recording. However, an examiner will be looking for an accurate lift. If you *do* add some of your own words – and you can – make sure that your words don't change the meaning, and that your answer makes sense as a whole.

Answers to Task 4

Questions 13–16

---

13   Three months/3 months

👤 Examiner Feedback

Other sample answers that would be accepted for question 13:

✓ 3 month – Yes, as this shows that you have understood the time and the measurement (the lack of the plural form wouldn't matter here).

Answers that an examiner would not accept, and why:

✗ 3 m – No, because this abbreviation is not standard for months. It could be millions or miles, but not months. It is a good idea to revise some basic abbreviations. It's also advisable to write responses in full, for example 'three months' (and not, for example, '3 mths').

✗ day release/one day a week – No, as this is her current arrangement, of one day's attendance each week. Look at the tense of the question: has Farida been – it's in the present perfect tense.

**14   One day (a week)/Every Wednesday/
(She attends the college) once a week**

👤 Examiner Feedback

Other sample answers that would be accepted for question 14:

✓ She is at a day weekly – Yes, because the main idea is that she is there on a one day a week arrangement. You have used your own words and it is clumsy English but the words don't lose the meaning. You located the specific detail of one day spent at college. However, as we have said, in Task 4, try to use the exact words from the recording.

Answers that an examiner would not accept, and why:

✗ (to be) an apprentice – No, because this is not a specific time commitment. An apprenticeship could last a year or be perhaps five years.

✗ to learn as she goes along – No, because this doesn't convey a specific response to *how often*.

---

15   Any three of:

- Analysed (the) parts
- Pressed the start (buttons)/Started them
- Carried them/Helped to carry them
- Listened to the noise they made

Examiner Feedback

Other sample answers that would be accepted for question 15:

✓ analysed them – Yes, this would be enough to convey the main idea of the specific detail.

✓ helped her dad to start them – Yes, but this would mean that you are inferring – working out what happened – and that is not needed in Task 4. But by adding this extra detail, the main idea remains – that she started them (but under her father's guidance).

✓ carry – Yes, it's the main idea of carrying that is needed.

Answers that an examiner would not accept, and why:

✗ part analysed them – No, this would be the wrong idea, so it changes the meaning. There is no evidence that Farida only partially analysed them.

✗ started to press them – No, as the main idea that Farida was allowed to start the drones is lost in this response. In fact, the idea of 'starting to press the drones' suggests something a much younger child would do to work out how they felt.

✗ care them – No. Is 'care' a misspelling of 'carry'? If so, this would be wrong as care in English is a common word meaning 'to look after'. If this answer means that Farida cared for them, there is no evidence of this, so it would be inferring too much.

16.1 • To get to difficult locations
• To access difficult places when it's too expensive to send in a crew (to film)

Examiner Feedback

Other sample answers that would be accepted for question 16.1:

✓ places where it's hard for a film crew to get to – Yes, as the use of your own wording is the same idea as in the recording.

✓ when the cost to send in a crew is high – Yes, as a 'high' cost means the same as expensive.

Answers that an examiner would not accept, and why:

✗ if a video team is not available – No, as this is much broader and brings in several ideas. Perhaps the team is not available for another reason, such as an operator being ill and not at work, or the team is away on training but they are needed to cover an immediate news story.

✗ when they don't have the money – No, as this also changes the meaning too much. The phrase 'don't have the money' is not synonymous with 'expensive'. Can you see why? These last two responses show how in Task 4 it's better to stay with the words and phrases on the recording and to try not to use your own words.

16.2 Rescue team

Examiner Feedback

Other sample answers that would be accepted for question 16.2:

✓ reskew team – Yes, as examiners are not checking accuracy of spelling in longer responses either.

Answers that an examiner would not accept, and why:

✗ Siberia – No, as this is given only as an example of a place where the drone would operate ('such as Siberia'). The drone is not designed specifically for people in Siberia. The key question word is *Who*. The answer is therefore going to be a person or people.

✗ a paramedic – No, as it's the rescue team who will actually use the drone. The paramedic will be called in later, if needed.

✗ victims of accidents/people stuck in cold and ice/patients/people who are lost – No, none of these can be accepted as there is no evidence that any would use the drone. They benefit from the use of the drone, but it's only the rescue team operators who use the drone, so Farida is making it for them. Remember, you are *listening for details* whilst all of the suggested answers above are inferences.

My score for Task 4	
What I found difficult	
What I have learnt	
Five ways I can improve	• _____ • _____ • _____ • _____ • _____

Transcript

Task 4

F1 Hi there. You're going to tell us about drones, aren't you? Those flying things that look like tiny helicopters that we are seeing more and more of, right?

F2 Hi. Yes, I will try, but to be honest I'm no expert. I started in the industry after leaving St John's college three months ago. I'm an apprentice, so I'm still learning as I go along. I'm doing a day release programme, so I spend every Wednesday at my new college.

F1 That's good to hear. Why drones? Did you have one when you were younger?

F2 Not exactly. My father has his own engineering company. When I was 11, he started to bring some drones home. At that age, he didn't trust me to fly them. I analysed the parts and pressed the start buttons. I loved the noise they made when they took off. Sometimes with dad's permission I carried the big ones. I remember one very large one. It was two metres wide if you include the rotor blades.

F1 The blades are the things on the top that rotate, aren't they? And they make the drone rise upward – just like a helicopter. We have a drone fitted with a video camera here at the radio station. We need it to access difficult locations. It's also useful when it's too expensive to send in a crew to film. Can you tell us more about the drones you work on?

F2 Well, actually, there's a wide range of uses. At the moment, we're designing a drone to be used in extremely cold temperatures and icy areas, such as Siberia. This drone is designed to carry a first aid kit. It will be used by a rescue team who can then decide how quickly a paramedic needs to be on the scene. It's equipped with a camera that can take images of bones, much like an X-ray machine does.

F1 Wow. There's more to drones than I thought.

Task 5

Now let's look at Task 5, and how it is structured in the Listening paper.

Common scenarios

Settings and scenarios that have appeared in previous exams include:

- a traveller talking about a month he spent in Beijing and the New Year Day activities that he took part in

- a doctor of science talking about how the increased use of plastic globally is causing great harm to nature, especially in the oceans where sea life is dying directly as a result of the number of plastic bags and bottles

- the founder of a charity talking about how global poverty is increasing and that the gap between the poorest people and the wealthiest is growing – his charity supports children in poverty by providing teaching materials and tutors

- a lecture given by a scientist about how the digital revolution has changed the way she uses technology in her research and how she has a virtual lab with hi-tech facilities inside her laptop using special software

- a presentation by a woman who works for a local council about maintaining the facilities for public use in her town – she is seeking volunteers to help for two hours a week. Volunteers will support the workers who are employed by the council to keep the town clean and running smoothly.

What do we notice about Task 5?

Task 5 is an extended monologue and has a formal tone. It is likely to be:

- a detailed talk or presentation that focuses on a single theme

- delivered by an adult speaker in a formal setting, such as a public meeting, a university lecture, or on a media channel.

What are the key assessment elements of Task 5?

Marks available	Number of words	How I will gain marks
8 marks – 5 questions worth either 1 or 2 marks each	broken into segments of 50–100 words – speaker is likely to use up about 300–400 words in 5 paragraphs of written text	• by identifying the key details from a range of short and longer texts (L1) • by identifying the overall message and key points in a variety of short and longer spoken texts, involving some more complex language (L2) • by recognising purpose, implied meaning, attitudes and feelings in extended texts (L4)

🔑 Key Points

There will be multiple-choice questions and open questions that ask you to write a response in your own words. You might also be asked to convey your understanding by providing a list of examples. There is likely to be a task that asks you to select true or correct statements from a list of 4–6.

Task 5 has a fuller range of questions than any of the other tasks, as it is intended to be the most challenging task in the examination. Therefore, simply repeating sentences from the recording is not likely to get you marks. What is being tested is your ability to understand overall ideas.

Language Support

To **infer** is to work out the meaning of something using clues and hints. You have to interpret and go beyond the information provided to come to a conclusion about what is meant. For example, if your brother tells you this, what can you conclude? "I couldn't get the eggs, sorry. I left it until today to go to the shop not realising it is a public holiday." We can conclude two things: 1) You asked him to buy eggs before today, and 2) Today the shop is closed as it's a holiday (so you didn't get your eggs).

To **deduce** is similar to 'infer' because you are coming to a conclusion based on details that you know. Think of it as coming to a logical conclusion given all of the evidence in front of you. It is slightly different from inferring because when deducing you might have all of the details, but you still need to make some sense of them. For example, what if your brother replied: "Today is a public holiday and the shop is closed. I know you asked me to go yesterday. Can't we make the pancakes without using eggs?" This time, we don't need to infer that the shop is closed, but we can deduce that he forgot about the public holiday as it's the most likely reason he didn't go yesterday.

Don't worry about this small difference between inference and deduction. The main thing is to think of them both as listening to what is implied by what people actually say, and working out the meaning by filling in the gaps or introducing something (inferring) or using logic to make sense of all the information you already have (deducing).

Assessment Objectives

L1, L2 and L4. You should be familiar now with L1 and L2. This task introduces L4, which tests your ability to listen for people's implied meaning, by recognising their attitudes and feelings. You will need to be clear about the speaker's purpose, and so be able to answer: Why have they chosen their topic and who is the intended audience? This will involve higher order skills, such as inference and deduction. We will practise these in this section.

Exam-style questions

Now let's explore Task 5 and the types of questions you are likely to be asked.

Mary Ong is the manager of an international airport. She is talking on a radio show about how her airport is working towards achieving smart status.

Pre-listening

You know from the description in the task who the speaker is and what the specific context is. So, what are the most important things to note?

- This is a formal talk given by one person and it focuses on international airports.
- Ask yourself: What do I know about how airports maintain safety?
- Do you know some useful vocabulary linked to airports?
- Also, what might the speaker mean by 'safer and smarter'? Is this perhaps to do with technology?
- What might the overall purpose be of this talk, which is on a radio show? Is Mary trying to persuade us of something?
- Remember that you need to think about attitudes and feelings in Task 5, so make sure to listen for how Mary *feels* about the topic.

Anticipating what will be spoken in an extended monologue is a really useful skill, especially in longer talks that stay on one topic and bring in several elements that relate closely to the overall message. Being able to follow the theme and see the 'bigger picture' will help you fill in some of the details.

Exam Tip

Remember, you shouldn't use all of the 5 minutes of preparation time reminding yourself what you know about the topic. Do this briefly but also use some of the time to look at each of the questions carefully. Using some prior knowledge to get a sense of what is being said or discussed is useful, but do not rely on it.

Try questions 17 to 21 without any guidance from us. However, don't worry, as we have provided plenty of feedback from the examiner after you have worked through the questions.

Now listen to the audio for **Task 5** on the website. You can listen to the recording twice.

Listen carefully to Mary's speech and then answer questions **17** to **21**.

17   What is Mary **not** going to talk about?

Write the correct letter in the box.

A	Progress being made
B	Selling holidays
C	Improvements

[1 mark]

18   Mary says that her organisation has a strong policy 'should anyone put on the line the welfare of others.'

Explain in your own words what this phrase means.   **[2 marks]**

_____

_____

_____

_____

19   Mary mentions what the airport has already done towards achieving smart status.

List **two** examples.   **[2 marks]**

1   _____

2   _____

20   What does Mary think about her IT staff?

Write the correct letter in the box.

A	They should get a bonus added to their salaries
B	They have lowered standards by working too fast
C	They deserve to be rewarded with a paid-for short break

[1 mark]

21 What are **two** points that Mary makes at the end of her talk?

Write the correct letters in the boxes.

A	Mary will conduct some interviews
B	People interviewed will be specially chosen
C	Mary is keen to get feedback about performance
D	Interviewers will be paid with free airline tickets
E	The aim is to carry out unbiased research
F	Interested people should contact the Research team

[ ] [ ]

[2 marks]

Revision Tip

There are two main ways that you can engage with a listening task. We call these 'top-down' and 'bottom-up'. The top-down approach means that you understand the smaller parts of the text based on your background knowledge and life experiences. For example, if a text is set in an airport, you can use your knowledge of what happens in an airport and the kind of language used in an airport to decode meaning. 'Decode' means to work out, sort out, and piece together an overall message. Bottom-up is when you try to understand individual words or phrases of the language and then build up a general understanding of the text.

You can develop these two approaches to help you prepare for the examination. To develop bottom-up listening skills, you can practise identifying sounds of words, syllables that are stressed in spoken common words, intonation patterns, grammatical forms that often feature in speech, such as contractions (for example, I'm, we're, they're, you're, don't, mustn't). It's also useful to learn the ways that people connect their speech, as linking words and phrases can be different from written English. For example, in speaking, you might say, "Sure, but we're going to the movies next." If you were writing this down, you might write a more formal, "However, our next stop is the cinema."

Take some time and listen again to some authentic recordings in English and think about how 'top-down' and 'bottom-up' can help to decode and understand what you are hearing. Also note how language can change between being spoken and written down.

Examiner feedback and raising my grade

How well did you do on Task 5? There are 8 marks available. Check your answers with the correct answers below. Note the feedback from the examiner to help you understand why a particular answer is correct and why some alternative answers are not correct.

Examiner Input

Task 5 has a mark scheme that covers three types of answers: multiple choice, a list of two items, and an open-ended answer. All of these have featured in Tasks 1 to 4, so there are no new question types that you need to prepare for.

Examiner Input

In Task 5, you will need to use higher level thinking skills to answer questions. For example, you may need to work out what a speaker is implying. You may come across some vocabulary that you don't know and have to use the surrounding words and context to work out what new words might mean. Also, you might be asked to say *in your own words* what someone else has said – and this requires you to process key points and an overall message so you can convey the same detail and idea.

Examiners are fully aware of this more difficult challenge and will always try to reward marks where they can. But also, please recognise that Tasks 4 and 5 are intended to be more challenging, in order to differentiate – that is, test stronger skills. Just keep practising!

Answers to Task 5

Questions 17–21

17	B

Examiner Feedback

It is clear that Mary is indeed going to focus on the other two areas later in her talk. She makes it very clear from the beginning that she is not selling anything.

18 Example answers:
- Takes chances with the safety of colleagues/other people
- Careless actions that fail to consider the safety of colleagues/other people

Examiner Feedback

The overall message here is that the organisation will act swiftly on a staff member who puts other people at risk of accidents or being unsafe. A firm policy means that there will be no second chances. However, you only need to say what the shorter phrase means and it has two parts: to not take chances or risks + always consider the safety of others. If you have one of these, then you will receive 1 mark, but for 2 marks you need to show you have understood both points.

Examiner Feedback

'Put on the line' is an idiom that means to take risky actions in the hope of getting a desired result. However, it can result in not succeeding. 'Cutting corners' is another idiom that can be used in this context. For example, 'staff who cut corners might be putting their colleagues' safety on the line'.

Answers that an examiner would not accept and the reason why:

✗ tries to look after the well fare of others – No, because this shows two things: that welfare has been misheard and it's the opposite idea of not considering other people's safety.

✗ takes a chance that others will fare well – No, as the message is not the same. Taking a chance that others will be okay is not what is happening – the person is not really considering the impact of their actions on others.

---

19   Criteria already met:
    1   Accessibility for people/for all/for everyone
    2   Queuing/waiting for less than/no more than 60 minutes

---

Examiner Feedback

Question 19 asks you to provide a list of two things. Remember not to write more than two things and also don't write outside the lines. The examiner will accept and mark only the first two items you offer. You don't need to use exactly the same words that Mary uses as for Task 5 – it's the overall message that matters as well as the specific detail. There will be a range of responses that examiners are likely to reward and mark as correct as long as what you write includes the key point and covers the overall message.

Answers that an examiner would not accept and the reason why:

✗ servicing 11 million passengers – No, because this is not a target set to achieve smart status.

✗ 24/7 – Again no, as this is a statement of fact rather than a target.

✗ Ensuring enough space for people – No, because Mary actually says that they have not met this smart status target yet.

✗ Not having to queue/wait – No, because this is not actually true. There will still be queues, but they will be less than 60 minutes. A response that stated 'shorter queues' would also be wrong, as it lacks the specific detail of 60 minutes.

✗ accessible four people – No, and this is mishearing 'for people' as 'four people'. It is wrong, because Mary is talking about accessibility for everyone.

20 C

Examiner Feedback

Because Task 5 is assessing the L4 objective, you are likely to be asked about the speaker's attitude and/or feelings. Answer B is interesting, because it is a reasonable inference to make if people do things too quickly. However, this would be your prior knowledge or opinion and not your new knowledge of what Mary has reported. There is no evidence of the IT working team going too quickly – just that they were quick to get to 95% of the target. Answer A is also reasonable, but money is not mentioned at all. If there is no evidence of a detail in a suggested answer in a multiple choice question then it will not be the correct answer. Note that the correct answer C rephrases 'free weekend return flight' to 'paid-for short break'.

21 C and E

Examiner Feedback

In Task 5, you may see a multiple-choice question that has up to six possible answers. Approach this in exactly the same way as you would a question with three answers. Task 5 is not asking you to collate or organise (L3), so focus on reading each suggested answer as its own standalone message or key point.

Here is the reason answers A, B, D, and F are wrong.

A – It's not Mary who will conduct the interviews. It is people interviewed by the Human Resources team who will appoint approved people, and who will then conduct the interviews.

B – The people interviewed with be chosen at random. So there is no special status or special selection criteria.

D – Interviewers will be paid, yes, but it is a fee (money). You may have heard 'free' and not 'fee'.

F – Listening carefully tells us that it's the Human Resources team that needs to be contacted.

My score for Task 5	
What I found difficult	
What I have learnt	
Six ways I can improve	• • • • • •

F1 Good afternoon, my name is Mary Ong. Thanks for inviting me on to your show to talk about our airport. I'm not here to advertise any holidays we have for sale. No, I'm here to focus on how we, like many other airports globally, are constantly trying to improve. We have a big aim at the moment and that is to achieve a high level of operations called smart status. Today, I will tell you about the progress we are making towards being a smart status airport here in Asia.

F1 We all want travelling by air to be quicker, safer, and less stressful. Safety is our number-one criterion. We have a one hundred per cent safety record for all flights departing and arriving – there have been no aircraft incidents reported at all. This also covers safety on the runways where we have thousands of staff doing things like maintenance, transporting luggage, and moving cargo. We have a firm safety policy that our staff know well should anyone put the welfare of others on the line.

F1 Our airport terminal services 11 million passengers a month, so we are a very busy place, 24/7. To reach smart status an airport must be fully accessible for people and we now satisfy this. We always know how many people are in the terminal at any one time, and we try to ensure enough space for crowds not to form. However, we are not quite there with that. A smart status airport must not have a queue in any part of the building that takes longer than 60 minutes. We are pleased to have achieved this target.

F1 On the technical side, we have invested millions of dollars in upgrading our communication systems. It's a requirement for smart status that all systems use fibre-optic cabling to ensure high-speed data transfer. Two weeks ago, we reached 95 per cent of that target. I was really pleased with how quickly they got there, so we plan to treat our entire IT workforce to a free weekend break and return flight in the Asian region, and we will allow them to leave work early on Friday at lunchtime.

F1 Another reason I'm here is to tell you that I'm fully behind our HR team who are looking for some people to check our performance by conducting random interviews of passengers and employees. This is not volunteer work. We will pay a fee to approved people to carry out this research for us. We don't want to use people already employed by us, because we want to keep things impartial. Anyone interested, please check our website and contact our Human Resources team for an application form.

Reflecting on progress made and reaching higher levels

In this unit, you have had guided practice at completing a full Listening paper with the aim of learning more about the skills you need to increase your performance in the examination. We have helped you strengthen your knowledge of what is required, we have recapped the key skills and assessment objectives, and you have applied these skills and your knowledge to help you feel confident and ready for the Listening paper.

On page 44 we asked you to estimate your levels of skills that are important to doing well in the exam. The table is repeated below. Don't look back at your original levels just yet – fill out the table below. Then compare the two tables and note what has changed.

Key skills	I think I need to improve in this area	I'm already quite good at this
Working out the overall meaning (the gist) of short statements		
Understanding the gist when more complex language is spoken		
Working out the overall message of longer talks when a single person is speaking		
Working out and organising the messages when more than one speaker is involved		
Listening for and locating specific details and information		
Understanding spoken Standard English		
Being familiar with the vocabulary – the words and phrases – used by speakers with different purposes		
Recognising when different tenses are used together – the relationship between past, present, and future events		
Recognising when a speaker gives an opinion		
Recognising when a speaker shows their feelings and attitudes in telling longer accounts		
In abstract scenarios and longer accounts, being able to infer what speakers are implying		

This is a reflective exercise and we want you to think about where you have improved.

- Do you feel that you have been able to recap all of the main skills needed for the Listening paper?

- Are you feeling confident about the range of themes and topics that you might be listening to?

- Do you have a good understanding now of how the Listening paper is constructed and how the questions are set?

If the answers to those questions are positive, then you are well on the way to success.

What do I need to know about the Speaking test?

You will hopefully have had some practice at how to approach the Speaking test during your English studies at school. The good news is that the structure of the test is straightforward and you will be able to take part in a discussion about general matters, sharing your thoughts, views, and opinions on a wide range of topics. You should approach the test as a chance to show your speaking skills and not be nervous about talking about the right content. Your teacher is likely to be the person who guides you through the two parts of the test. Speak freely, and try to enjoy the experience!

The Speaking test approaches the themes and topics in this way:

- In Part 1, on the Photo card, you will see the topic you have to talk about. In the list on page 90, we list some of the topics covered in Part 1 in some previous examination sessions.

- Part 2, the General conversation, will focus on the themes NOT used in the Photo card.

Here is a table of the themes and topics.

Theme one: Identity and culture	**Topic 1: Me, my family, friends and people I know** • Relationships with family • Relationships with friends and people I know **Topic 2: Technology in everyday life** • Social media • Mobile technology **Topic 3: Free-time activities** • Music • Cinema and TV • Sport • Customs and festivals
Theme two: Local, national, international and global areas of interest	**Topic 1: Home, town, neighbourhood and region** **Topic 2: Social issues** • Charity/voluntary work • Healthy/unhealthy living **Topic 3: Global issues** • The environment • Poverty **Topic 4: Travel and tourism**

Theme three: Current and future study and employment	**Topic 1: My studies**
	Topic 2: Life at school/college
	Topic 3: Education post-16
	Topic 4: Jobs, career choices and ambitions

You can see that during the 10 minutes of the Speaking test, you might cover a range of topics – you should be prepared to talk about all of the topics above, but of course your conversation with the examiner might not include them all.

You need to know:

* the structure of the Speaking test and its two parts, so that you are fully prepared for the format and there will be no surprises

* the way that the themes and topics and covered (more on this later)

* how to deal with the Photo card which is the first part of the test

* the transition to the General conversation which is the second part of the test

* how best to respond to the prompts and questions throughout

* what you can expect from your teacher who is conducting the test

* how the examiner – who the full recorded test is sent to – will assess your test.

As you work through each of the practice Photo cards in the Apply section below, we will help you to develop your speaking skills, including communicating clearly, improving your conversation and discussions, speaking spontaneously, and varying your spoken language.

Assessment objectives: Speaking

Communicate and interact in speech

S1: Communicate clearly using speech appropriate to situation and audience.

S2: Make appropriate and accurate use of a variety of vocabulary and grammatical structures.

S3: Produce extended sequences of speech, answering and, as appropriate, asking questions, and expressing opinions with spontaneity and fluency.

S4: Demonstrate appropriate pronunciation and intonation.

Recap

What are the key skills I will need for success in the Reading Paper?

Let's recap the key skills using the specification and explore what they mean:

"Communicate and interact effectively in speech for a variety of purposes, using and adapting language appropriately."

What does this mean for you?

- **Communicate and interact effectively:** This means to be able to say clearly what you think so that your listener understands what you say and can respond if necessary. You will be having a two-way discussion.

- **Variety of purposes:** When we are speaking, what we say depends on the situation. We could be giving directions, suggesting a great film to watch, answering a question from a parent, criticising a sports team we love when they play badly – it's a long list of situations! In the test, your focus or purpose is less wide-ranging. In the first part, when you discuss the Photo card the teacher will use the second and third questions to generate a conversation about the situation shown on the card. In the second part the purpose is to have a more general discussion.

- **Adapting language appropriately:** Remember that the test is a formal test and you should be using an appropriate style of spoken language. It's not a good idea to use spoken slang language in the test. However, there are times in a discussion when informality is good and it flows naturally. At this stage, be aware that you need to change your language to suit the discussion and not attempt to stay in one prepared style. In other words, don't be too formal as this isn't normal in a conversation.

"Develop skills in conversation by responding to questions and exchanging opinions."

What does this mean for you?

The test lasts about 10 minutes. It starts with your description of a photograph, but very quickly turns into a conversation. You will respond to three questions from the teacher in Part 1, and in Part 2 a fuller discussion develops. You can share opinions on the themes and topics, so be ready to have some opinions.

"Convey information and narrate events coherently and confidently, using and adapting language for new purposes."

What does this mean for you?

Remember that AQA encourage you to develop your speaking skills for the whole of your course of study and not just for an exam. Your teachers will have helped you to narrate events and will have increased your confidence to speak for longer periods. This will have helped you to prepare for the times in the test when you have to speak for longer.

- **New purposes:** In the test, however, you shouldn't worry about new purposes. This unit's practice will prepare you for this.

> "Speak spontaneously, responding to unexpected questions, points of view or situations, sustaining communication as appropriate"

What does this mean for you?

The key part of this skill is to be able to respond naturally to the points, views, opinions, and ideas that arise in a normal discussion. In the test, there are only two of you taking part in the conversation – an examiner (who is likely to be your teacher) and yourself. It's a two-way discussion.

- **Spontaneously:** This is an adjective which also means unplanned and unrehearsed. Think of it as responding to unexpected questions that follow on from your last answer. It follows therefore that if you try to plan and prepare a spoken response for the test, and try to insert it, you are unlikely to do well.

- **Sustaining communication:** 'sustained' means continuing for an extended period without interruption. There are times when you should talk for longer, whether to state your own point or idea, or to respond to the teacher, and this will help you perform better in the test.

> "Initiate and develop conversations and discussion, producing extended sequences of speech."

What does this mean for you?

'To initiate' means to cause something to begin. For the test, it means that at times, if you are confident, you can start a discussion point. However, it's probably more important to develop the point by being involved in a two-way conversation about it. You should keep your points 'on track' and not move to something completely different – that's not what 'developing' it means.

- **Extended sequences of speech:** We have already mentioned that you will need to talk for longer at times. An 'extended sequence' means that you should stay focused on the topic or issue being discussed, passing ideas about it between you and the teacher. It's talking for longer but with a clear flow – this should result in a fluent conversation.

> "Make appropriate and accurate use of a variety of vocabulary and grammatical structures, including some more complex forms, with reference to past, present and future events."

What does this mean for you?

By the time you get to the test you will know the level of your spoken language in terms of the extent of your vocabulary, and how accurate and varied your grammar is. It's probably not a good idea to experiment with vocabulary and grammar in the test. Yes, demonstrate your knowledge of words, and yes, be sure to talk about events in a range of tenses. To achieve complex forms, speaking for longer periods with a clear purpose should help. But we suggest you stay in your comfort zone and concentrate on making clear points and taking part in a relevant discussion.

> "Make creative and more complex use of the language, as appropriate, to express and justify their own thoughts and points of view."

What does this mean for you?

These are higher level speaking skills. You may find that you are over-stretched in trying to speak in more complex language. Our advice is do not over-stretch. It is better to remain comfortable in the test and keep talking at a level you are confident with. Longer pauses, when you stop speaking to think of more complex language, are not a good idea. It is fine to pause to think about an idea, but don't pause for too long!

Creative: This doesn't mean, for example, telling a story or a joke. It means talking in a way that uses fluent and expressive language, perhaps using some similes and metaphors. However, a short account of an event – called an anecdote – is fine. But keep anecdotes short and relevant to the idea being discussed.

Justify: If you say something that is your thought, your idea, or your opinion, go on to explain why. You can do this by adding more detail and giving examples. This will help you develop the discussion – a key skill already mentioned. Be aware that the teacher is probably going to ask you to justify an opinion, so be ready.

"Use accurate pronunciation and intonation to be understood by a native speaker."

What does this mean for you?

Your target in the Speaking test is to speak in such a way that a native speaker can understand you and have a discussion with you. When you need to use English in an English-speaking country you will meet people who have a range of pronunciation and intonation, and also people who speak with regional accents. The examiners are very aware of regional accents and these are fine.

Pronunciation: This is the way in which a word is spoken in English. Spelling does not determine this. The best way to achieve accurate pronunciation is to listen to how native speakers say (pronounce) the words. It's a good idea to listen to a lot of discussions between two people on a range of topics. This will help with intonation too.

Intonation: This is the rise and fall (the pitch) of the speaking voice. It can be a challenge as intonation changes depending on where people are from (for example, a whole country, but also regions within a country). Aim for standard intonation patterns. To understand the importance of intonation, think about how it sounds if you speak with no intonation – that is, in a monotone voice. Try it and you will see how unnatural this sounds. This is sometimes called robotic English – you sound like a robot – and it will affect the conversation.

Reflect

Reflecting on my current speaking skills

Complete the table below right now with an estimate of your current skills. Just tick the box that you feel is closest to your level. That's all you need to do at the moment. We will return to this later.

Key skills	I think I need to improve in this area	I'm already quite good at this
Saying clearly what I'm thinking so that my listeners understand me		
Adapting/changing my speaking for different situations – for example, to be more formal when required		
Sharing my opinions		
Being confident in responding to questions, prompts, and ideas from other people		
Narrating well and talking for longer to describe a photograph or an event to someone		
Being spontaneous and responding quickly to unexpected questions		
Being good at extending a conversation on the same topic and playing my role to keep a discussion going and focused		
Using higher level skills, such as being creative with language		
Justifying what I say by adding reasons for views and opinions		
Being happy with how I sound in terms of: a) pronunciation b) intonation (to be easily understood by a native speaker)		

Apply

What is the best way for me to apply this knowledge and these skills to practise for the Speaking test?

Part 1 – Photo card

Let's start with Part 1 of the Speaking test, where you are shown a Photo card.

Common scenes and topics

Scenes that have appeared in previous tests include:

- a young boy surrounded by his family who are all celebrating his birthday – the topic is **customs and festivals**

- a group of four friends, probably students, with a book and a laptop – the topic is **relationships with friends and people I know**

- a customer making a payment in a cafe – the topic is **mobile technology**

- four adults out running, taking part in exercise together – the topic is **sport**

- a family with two young children having a picnic outside – the topic is **relationships with family**

- a man playing a guitar behind a young boy who is using upturned cooking pans as drums – the topic is **music**

- three young women watching television, eating popcorn, and all having the same surprised look – the topic is **cinema and TV**

- three adults and a young girl preparing food in a kitchen and taking a selfie – the topic is **mobile technology**.

As you can see, the Photo card in Part 1 is likely to show a small group of people, friends, or family, taking part in a regular activity. However, it may feature only one person. The setting can arise from any of the themes and topics in the specification.

Part 2 – General conversation

This part takes about 6 to 7 minutes and will cover the themes not covered in Part 1. In our sample, this means that because Theme one: Identity and culture was covered in Part 1, the General conversation (Part 2) will be based around both of the remaining two themes. Both themes will be covered equally, so you can expect about 3 minutes' discussion around each. Don't worry, you will know when this part starts as you will hear 'Now, the General conversation is beginning with the theme of …' or something similar.

So what type of questions should you expect? Examples of Part 2 questions for all three themes are listed below. But note that the teacher does not have to use any of these. Their role is to support you and help guide you to a successful conversation. You might spend more time discussing one topic in depth if this shows your speaking strength. However, you might cover a wider range of topics if it helps you keep the conversation going.

Theme one: Identity and culture

- What is your ideal family?

- What do you like doing with your family?

- What have you done with your friends recently?

- How do you use social media to keep in contact with your friends?

- What are the best uses for mobile technology?

- How does music enrich the lives of people?

- What is the best film you have seen at the cinema? Why?

- Why do you think so many people like to play sport?

- How do you celebrate your birthday?

- Why is it important to continue local customs?

Theme two: Local, national, international and global areas of interest

- What is there for young people to do in the area where you live?

- What could you do to be a good neighbour?

- Which charity do you think most deserves support? Why?

- What are the best ways to keep fit and healthy?

- What are the main problems faced by homeless people?

- What are the effects of global warming?

- Why do you think so many people like to visit other countries?

- Where would you most like to go for a holiday? Why?

Theme three: Current and future study and employment

- Which subject do you most enjoy studying? Why?

- Explain why it is important to learn other languages.

- What could be done to improve your life in school/college?

- In your opinion, what makes a good teacher?

- What do you plan to study next year?

- What could be the advantages of going to university?

- Would you like to work in England? Why/why not?

- Describe your ideal job.

What are the key assessment elements of the Speaking test?

Marks available	Time taken	How I will gain marks
Photo card – 15 marks General conversation – 25 marks Total marks: 40	3–4 minutes 6–7 minutes	For Part 1: • by communicating clearly using speech appropriate to situation and audience (S1) • by making appropriate and accurate use of a variety of vocabulary and grammatical structures (S2) For Part 2, in addition to S1 and S2 above: • by producing extended sequences of speech, answering and, as appropriate, asking questions, and expressing opinions with spontaneity and fluency (S3) • by demonstrating appropriate pronunciation and intonation (S4)

Key Points

In Part 1 you are given a Photo card. It will show a scene, involving a small group of people, or perhaps one or two people. Your task is to talk about the picture – which is the first bullet point. Next, there are two questions that relate to the context of the theme and topic, not just the picture. You will have had some time to think about the scene and prepare for Part 1.

The Photo card is selected by the teacher – you do not have a choice. The teacher uses a specified set order, so they do not have a choice of Photo card either.

Assessment Objectives

S1 and S2. Part 1 asks you to describe and talk about a photograph. You can see the assessment criteria above. Note that in Part 1, you are not assessed on S3 or S4, so don't worry about pronunciation and intonation. However, you do need to talk clearly, communicate efficiently, and be accurate in your grammar and use of words.

Now let's explore an example of Part 1 and a Photo card. Before you look at anything else in this section, take 10 minutes and do some preparation for the test. For practice, find a partner such as a friend, sibling, or parent and ask them to ask you questions on each photo card. Record your answers to all the questions and show them to your teacher for them to mark.

Exam-style questions

! Exam Tip

You could write some notes about this Photo card to help you. Do not write in full sentences as this may lead to you wanting to read them out in full. The notes should be brief and used as prompts for what you are going to say. Speaking naturally is what is required.

Theme one   Card A Photo card

*   Look at the photo during the preparation period.

*   Make any notes you wish to on an additional answer sheet.

*   Your teacher will then ask you questions about the photo and about topics related to **Relationships with family**.

Your teacher will ask you the following **three** questions:

*   What can you see in the photo?

*   What do you like to do together as a family?

*   Why is it important to go outside with members of your family?

[15 marks]

👤 Examiner Input

This Photo card focuses on Theme one: Identity and culture. This means that in Part 1 you could be talking about three topics. This topic is about you, your friends, and people you know, and, specifically, the relationships people have with their family. The other two topics you might be asked about in Theme one are technology in everyday life, and free-time activities.

Exam Tip

The teacher will ask you the three questions on the Photo card in order. If you don't understand a question fully you can ask for it to be paraphrased. For example, for these sample questions, you could ask for a clarification of 'to go outside'. You may be told that it also means 'to do activities away from the home'. At all times, your teacher will try to support you and help keep the flow going, so don't be shy to ask for things to be clarified. But remember, they cannot do the exam for you, so don't expect them to fill in any gaps with the right vocabulary or to correct your grammar.

Exam Tip

You will also be asked more questions – not just the ones on the Photo card. This is to help the teacher continue the conversation. However, they can use any questions they want to that relate to the topic. In our sample, you could expect some of these questions:

- Tell me about where the people are exactly.
- What time of year do you think it is?
- How often do you go out as a family?
- What are some of your favourite places?
- Who do you get on especially well with in your family?
- Why do you get on so well with him or her?
- What are their best qualities?

Can you think of two more questions you are likely to be asked?

1 _____

_____

2 _____

_____

Exam Tip

Whilst it's a good idea to revise vocabulary and phrases to prepare for the Speaking test, be very careful not to include too many of these pre-learnt phrases in the test, just because you have learnt them. Doing this can result in an unnatural conversation, sometimes called stilted language – that is, stiff, awkward, unrelaxed. Avoid this and keep your speech flowing and as natural as you can.

Revision Tip

Remember that in Part 1, you are only assessed for communication, and knowledge and use of language. There's no need to over-stretch yourself. It's best to stay in your comfort zone and not attempt to 'drop in' segments of practised spoken language because you have learnt them. Both parts of the exam involve developing a conversation, and this works best when it's natural and flowing. Avoid discussion which becomes 'laboured' (hard work), and artificial. Keep it flowing and, if necessary, use more straightforward language that you are comfortable with.

Revision Tip

Remember that you don't need to be able to speak uninterrupted for a long time to do well in the Speaking test. It's discussion that is encouraged. Try to practise short and focused discussions to help build your confidence. For example, with a friend, parent, teacher, or older sibling choose one of the topics from pages 90–91 above and take part in a two-way discussion, each of you asking and answering questions.

Revision Tip

Try to find photos that relate to the themes and topics from the Specification – remember that any of the themes could be part of your Speaking test. Talk about the photo for about two minutes to a friend, or a family member. They can then ask questions related to the photo for you to answer.

Theme two   Card B Photo card

- Look at the photo during the preparation period.

- Make any notes you wish to on an additional answer sheet.

- Your teacher will then ask you questions about the photo and about topics related to **Healthy/unhealthy living**.

Your teacher will ask you the following **three** questions:

- What can you see in the photo?

- What do you like to do to keep yourself healthy?

- Why is it important to exercise regularly?

[15 marks]

Theme three   Card C Photo card

- Look at the photo during the preparation period.

- Make any notes you wish to on an additional answer sheet.

- Your teacher will then ask you questions about the photo and topics related to **Jobs, career choices and ambitions**.

Your teacher will ask you the following **three** questions.

- What can you see in the photo?

- What activities do you like to do using your hands?

- What are the benefits of working in science?

[15 marks]

Examiner Input

Effective preparation does not mean memorising pre-prepared answers. This is very obvious to the examiner who will mark your performance and it will affect your marks for spontaneity and fluency.

Examiner Input

It's not enough to just offer an opinion in a discussion. Remember to justify your opinions.

Revision Tip

Revision Tip

Work with a partner and ask each other some questions about your performance:

- Did I reply to all questions?
- How well did I develop my responses?
- How clear and extensive were my explanations?
- How effective and complex were my language choices?
- Was my use of language accurate?
- Did I use any subordinate clauses?
- Was I able to speak for extended periods?
- How clearly did I communicate my ideas?
- Did I accurately use the past, present, and future tense?

Revision Tip

Ask your teacher for exemplars (examples of good Speaking tests), examiner commentaries, and study the mark scheme to help deepen your understanding of the expectations of the Speaking test.

Revision Tip

Using PREP. Look at this example of how to develop a conversation.

Point	Practise using one-sentence responses to a question.	'I do some running every day to keep fit.'
Reason	Offer a short explanation of why you do this.	'I feel that this makes me keep my heart and body healthy.'
Example	Here you add some context to your reason. You can also vary your use of tenses. See how the past tense is used in the example.	'Last year I entered a 5km run and I was out of breath at half-way! I promised myself then that I would work on my fitness levels.'
Point	A follow-up sentence might give you the chance to use advanced English – such as modal verbs.	'If I am going to be a tennis player, which is my aim in life, then I should build up my heart and stamina now.'

Try this PREP. An opening short sentence is given for you to build on.

Point	"When I get a job and work, I'd like to work in the airline industry."
Reason	_____ _____ _____
Example	_____ _____ _____
Point	_____ _____ _____

Reflecting on progress made and reaching higher levels

In this unit, you have had guided practice at preparing for the Speaking test with the aim of learning more about the approach and skills you need to increase your performance. We have helped you strengthen your knowledge of what is required, we have recapped the key skills and assessment objectives, and you have engaged with these skills to help you feel confident and ready for the Speaking test.

On page 89 we asked you to estimate your levels of skills that are important to doing well in the exam. The table is repeated below. Don't look back at your original levels just yet – fill out the table below. Then compare the two tables and note what has changed.

Key skills	I think I need to improve in this area	I'm already quite good at this
Saying clearly what I'm thinking so that my listeners understand me		
Adapting/changing my speaking for different situations – for example, to be more formal when required		
Sharing my opinions		
Being confident in responding to questions, prompts, and ideas from other people		
Narrating well and talking for longer to describe a photograph or an event to someone		
Being spontaneous and responding quickly to unexpected questions		
Being good at extending a conversation on the same topic and playing my role to keep a discussion going and focused		
Using higher level skills, such as being creative with language		
Justifying what I say by adding reasons for views and opinions		
Being happy with how I sound in terms of: a) pronunciation b) intonation (to be easily understood by a native speaker)		

This is a reflective exercise and we want you to think about where you have improved.

- Do you feel that you have been able to recap all of the main skills needed for the Speaking test?

- Are you feeling confident about the range of themes and topics that you might be talking about?

- Do you have a good understanding now of how the Speaking test is constructed and how the tasks are set?

If the answer to those questions is positive, then you are well on the way to success.

Knowledge

What do I need to know about the Writing paper?

You will be familiar with the writing tasks that you are asked to do for the examination. Your teachers will have given you plenty of practice in writing to inform, explain, describe, persuade, and so on, so there should be no surprises in terms of writing in a certain way and for a specified audience. You will probably be writing about topics such as friends/family, your school, the environment, modern technology, staying healthy, and volunteer work – in other words, themes and topics that you know about and have probably had experience with.

Theme one – Identity and culture

Theme two – Local, national, international and global areas of interest

Theme three – Current and future study and employment

You need to know:

- the structure of the Writing paper, including how the tasks are laid out, so that you are fully prepared for the examination and there will be no surprises

- the themes and topics that occur in specific tasks, to help you predict what to expect

- how you are expected to write down your responses, including the number of words you are expected to write

- how to deal with any photographs that are provided as a stimulus for writing

- how you will be assessed by the examiners – in other words, where you will gain marks and how best to optimise this to raise your grade

- the balance of the four tasks, and how much time to spend on each, given the marks available.

You will develop your writing skills by working through the practice questions and reading the relevant features like those listed in the 'How to use this book' section on pages v–vi. Writing skills, of course, include accurate grammar, spelling, punctuation, syntax, and structures.

Assessment objectives: Writing

Communicate in writing

W1: Write short texts to convey meaning and exchange information.

W2: Produce clear and coherent text of extended length to present key points, details and ideas.

W3: Make accurate use of vocabulary and grammatical structures; spell and punctuate accurately.

W4: Manipulate the language with increasing fluency and creativity for a variety of purposes.

Recap

What are the key skills I will need for success in the Writing paper?

Let's recap the key skills using the specification and explore what they mean:

"Communicate effectively in writing for a variety of purposes across a range of specified contexts."

What does this mean for you?

- **Communicate effectively:** This means writing In a clear way that matches your ability level. In other words, don't try to be over-complex, as the more you stretch yourself the more likely it is that you will make errors that could affect what you are trying to communicate to your reader(s). If the reader can read your whole piece, fairly quickly and smoothly, and understand your main message, then you have communicated effectively.

- **Variety of purposes:** You should recognise the specific purpose of the writing by identifying the clues in the prompt. For example, if you were asked about a photograph of a busy market square, your purpose would be to describe what people are doing. Other purposes are to inform, to explain, to narrate (tell a story), to entertain, to persuade, to argue, to analyse, to appeal – and more. Be sure that you are clear about your purpose when writing, even for a shorter piece of 30–50 words.

- **Specified contexts:** This is good news, as it means you will always be given the context, and from this you will get some idea about your intended audience. For example, if the context is to organise an event in your school's computer room then you will probably need to write to your computing teacher first. That teacher might then ask you to write a different letter for a different audience – parents – as the context changes.

"Write short texts, using simple sentences and familiar language accurately to convey meaning and exchange information"

What does this mean for you?

The examination will test your skill at producing pieces of writing of different lengths, from 30 words to up to 150 words. When writing short texts, it's important to keep things simple and straightforward, to make sure you communicate clearly and accurately, so that your intended meaning is understood.

- **Familiar language:** This is also good news, as it means you don't need to impress an examiner with sophisticated language all the time. It's important to be able to use everyday words and expressions, and of course without too many errors. 'Familiar' means that it's known by most people who use the language daily.

- **Exchange information:** Just to be clear, this does not mean that in your exam you are actually exchanging written pieces. However, if you are asked to write to inform or describe, you are passing on information and details from yourself to the other person, so it is a kind of exchange. Always keep your reader(s) in mind, as this will improve your written work. For example, if your task is to write an email, it is likely the email will be read very quickly and a response is also quite likely. Being aware of this exchange will make your writing more direct and concise.

"Produce clear and coherent text of extended length to present facts and express ideas and opinions appropriately for different purposes and in different settings."

What does this mean for you?

- **Extended length:** This means a piece of writing that can be up to 150 words. Note that the word counts increase with each task so your writing becomes longer and more extended each time. In longer pieces of writing you are likely to have facts, opinions, ideas, and other details, so the challenge is to organise and present these so that your reader can follow clearly what you are saying. Word counts are guidelines so it's best to stay within them but the examiners will not penalise you (take marks away from you) if your writing goes over the word count.

- **Different settings:** Settings are the situations during the course in which you write – for example, for an exam, for classwork, as brief notes, or in a real world scenario. The setting might be given to you, but in some cases, you will be expected to choose the setting.

"Make accurate use of a variety of vocabulary and grammatical structures, including some more complex forms, to describe and narrate with reference to past, present and future events."

What does this mean for you?

By the time you get to the examination – and probably also by the time you are using this *Revision Guide* – you will have reached a certain level with your grammar, vocabulary, and syntax (your use of a range of sentences). At this stage, therefore, don't worry about learning a lot of new vocabulary and new grammatical skills. It's more important that you refine (improve carefully) your existing knowledge and skills by practising appropriate writing. In other words, it's important to become better at what you are already good at.

- **Vocabulary:** The examiner wants to see a range of words being used but being used appropriately. Try not to repeat words, therefore, but think of other words that help clarify your intended meaning. It's useful to have a good knowledge of words that go together with each other. These are called 'semantic fields'. For example, think of words that are associated with travel, and you will see that you already know many. A semantic field that is very specific – for example computer words – is called 'jargon'. Varying your vocabulary is important if you are aiming for higher marks.

- **Structures:** In English language, structures are how you arrange and relate (connect) the different elements of your piece of writing. This can be at paragraph level, so making sure each paragraph links to the previous one and each paragraph is a complete whole. It can also mean how accurate your sentences are and how well you develop sentences, for example, using connecting words (connectives) and subordinate clauses. Good structure is the use of a range of sentence types and how well they fit together.

To show that you have control over whether your writing is focusing on the past, the present, or the future – or a combination – you will need to use a range of verbs in accurate tenses, and for the future, appropriate qualifiers depending on when the action is taking place. We will help you improve these skills in the sample answers provided later in this unit.

> *"Manipulate the language, using and adapting a variety of structures and vocabulary with increasing accuracy and fluency for new purposes, including using appropriate style and register."*

What does this mean for you?

- **Manipulate:** This is a higher level skill. 'Manipulate' means to handle or control words in a skilful way, sometimes by altering or changing them to be more effective given the task in hand. If you can manipulate language, you will have a high level of confidence as you will be able to adapt structures and use words in a skilful way to clarify and extend meaning.

- **Style:** This is the way something is written. Think of style as the language – words and grammar – that people choose to suit the circumstances. The style of spoken and written language therefore depends on why you are speaking or writing.

- **Register:** Think of register on a sliding scale from very formal to quite casual. If you are writing for a court of law, for example, this is a very formal register. If you are sending a text message to a close friend, this is very informal. An appropriate register will come from the specified audience and context.

For your written exam pieces, it's more important that you identify how formal or informal you need to be according to the purpose and context. Don't worry about style and register as technical terms because you will identify why you are writing and to whom, and your writing will naturally match this.

> *"Make independent, creative and more complex use of the language to explain, inform, describe, argue or persuade."*

What does this mean for you?

This is a really important skill to ensure success in your Writing paper. In the four tasks, you are likely to have explained, described, persuaded, argued, informed, and more! But let's have a closer look at two aspects of this.

- **Independent:** What this really means is that the examiner can see that you are confident in your own choice and use of words, grammar, and structures. You have not relied on remembering chunks (large pieces) of writing that have come from another context, or for another purpose. What you have done is looked at the specific task on the examination paper and responded directly to that – and this is when you will achieve competence. This is an important message that we will repeat in this unit: Don't copy or use writing from another source – be independent and write in your own words.

- **Creative:** Creativity is also a sign of confidence in your writing, and you certainly cannot rely on prepared or memorised writing to show your creative responses. What we mean by creative on the exam paper is to make your writing imaginative. For example, if you are asked to plan a music concert at a venue, you could use your school hall. However, creating a more interesting venue – for example, outdoors in the centre of an ancient city – might help your writing become more creative.

Reflecting on my current writing skills

Complete the table below right now with an estimate of your current skills. Just tick the box that you feel is closest to your level. That's all you need to do at the moment. We will return to this later.

Key skills	I think I need to improve in this area	I'm already quite good at this
Being clear about the purpose of my writing		
Keeping a strong focus on the audience – the reader(s) of my writing		
Choosing the correct style and register – do I have a wide range of types of writing?		
Being sure of the required setting and the broader context		
Using a wide range of vocabulary		
Using accurate spelling		
Using correct grammar, including verb tenses to indicate past, present, and future		
Using accurate structures, connecting words and phrases, and a range of different sentence types		
The amount of relevant detail given in longer pieces of writing		

Apply

What is the best way for me to apply this knowledge and these skills to practise for the Writing paper?

Task 1

Let's start with Task 1 on the Writing paper, where you are shown a photograph..

Common scenes

Locations and scenes that have appeared in previous exams include:

- a coastal scene with waves crashing onto the rocks and a single house in a field in the distance – taken from a holiday magazine

- a city scene of shops and cafes in front of old buildings with people walking in the street – taken from a magazine

- a cable car linking two mountain peaks with views of more peaks in the distance and a seaside town – taken from a travel website

- a city scene of a fruit and vegetable market with apartments in buildings above the market stalls and people in the street – taken from a travel blog

- a climber on a steep mountainside with other peaks and a lake behind showing how high up the climber is – taken from a tourism leaflet.

As you can see, the photograph in Task 1 is likely to show the natural beauty of our planet or in some cases scenes in our cities and towns. There may or may not be people visible in the picture. However, in two of the above cases we can certainly imagine people being there (in the distant house, and in the cable car). You are likely to be shown a photograph that functions at two levels: the immediate scene in front of you and any emotion or atmosphere that is conveyed as a whole.

What are the key assessment elements of Task 1?

Marks available	Number of words to write	How I will gain marks
9 marks – 1 task	30–50 words	• by writing a short text to convey meaning and exchange information (W1) • by spelling and punctuating accurately (part of W3)

Key Points

In Task 1, you are asked to describe. It is a short piece of writing – between 30 and 50 words – and it's important therefore that you do not try to incorporate another purpose or style of writing. You only need to focus on descriptive writing. You are given around ten lines on the exam paper and this is plenty to write 50 words, so please don't try to write outside the lines. And, of course, do a quick count of your words after you have written four or five lines.

Examiner Input

Task 1 has focused on Theme two and specifically Topic 4: Travel and tourism. However, other topics, such as customs and festivals (Theme one, Topic 3), the environment (Theme two, Topic 3) and healthy living (Theme two, Topic 2) could also be relevant as you look deeper into the setting and context of the photograph's location. But remember to describe the scene as you see it and not as you'd like it to be!

Assessment Objectives

W1 and (part of) W3. Task 1 is a short text of 30–50 words so your focus is on providing appropriate and acceptable information about the scene or location. Note that you are not assessed yet (you will be later in the exam) on the accuracy of your grammar and vocabulary. You are only assessed on the accuracy of your spelling and punctuation. It's important in Task 1 that you use full stops, commas, and apostrophes accurately.

Exam-style questions

Now let's explore an example of Task 1 and the style of descriptive writing required. Read the guidance on this page and at the top of the next page and then write your description of the photograph in question 01.

01 Look closely at this photograph from a travel guide.

Describe what you see in the photograph.

Your description should be between 30 and 50 words. **[9 marks]**

_____

_____

_____

_____

_____

_____

_____

_____

_____

! Exam Tip

You don't need to cover everything that is in the photo. Students have been very successful in Task 1 by focusing on a couple of main aspects and developing them with clear descriptive details.

Examiner Input

Each of the tasks suggests the number of words you should stay within. You will not be penalised or lose marks if you go over or slightly under the word counts. However, when students write more than they need to, it can result in unnecessary mistakes, which the examiner will look at. The examiner will read all of your writing and take into account all that you have written. Therefore, we recommend strongly you stay under the top limit. For Task 1, the top limit is 50 words. Be assured that you can gain full marks on each of the tasks by staying well inside the given words counts.

Task 1

_____

_____

_____

_____

_____

 Examiner Input

Remember that for the first writing task you do not need to use ambitious vocabulary and/or impressive grammar skills. You are only tested on spelling and punctuation. Therefore, it makes very good sense to keep your descriptions straightforward, and you can do this for full marks in 30–50 words. Aim for a clear piece of writing that doesn't have a delay in communication. Get your descriptions across quickly and directly. You can attempt more ambitious use of English later on in the Writing paper.

Language Support

1 Remember your **prepositions** to navigate the photo and to vary the use of these. For example: 'I see trees <u>near to</u> buildings and more buildings <u>close to</u> a river.'

2 Remember your **adjectives** to add specific detail. For example: 'The black building one side is a <u>sharp</u> contrast to the <u>brighter</u> buildings nearby.'

3 Use your words carefully and avoid using complex vocabulary. For example, 'the skyscrapers at the front are white and the trees in the park are dark green' is fine. If you try to suggest, for example, the skyscrapers are 'glistening' and the trees are 'verdant', you need to be confident and spell those words correctly. Don't overdo vocabulary for Task 1.

4 **Semantic fields**: It would be useful, for example, to have a good vocabulary about buildings. Some examples you could use in our Task 1 photograph are: 'roof', 'concrete', 'brick', 'steel', 'stone', 'traditional', 'futuristic', 'elaborate', 'breathtaking', 'tranquil', 'skyscraper'.

Examiner feedback and raising my grade

Now that you have written your response to Task 1, look at the three sample responses below, and the guidance, tips, and advice offered.

Achievement levels

We are going to use a method to mark each sample response that is very similar to the way that an examiner will assess your writing. For all of the tasks, there are two criteria:

- **Content and communication:** You can think of this as how clearly you have conveyed the content you have chosen to write about to your reader.
- **Language:** This is your accurate, appropriate, and varied use of words, phrases, punctuation, sentences, and structures.

For Task 1, there are four levels available for each criterion – Level 3 is the best/highest and Level 0 means that a response doesn't have enough merit to be awarded any marks at all. Here, let's focus on working at Levels 3, 2, and 1.

Sample answers to Task 1

Sample response – Student 1

> In the pictare is park and we went there two years ago in cold it is cold there I also see conkreet in front and insid I also see what it look like a river but in betwen that there is park, Park has few trees it is a beatifull view there.

Examiner Feedback

Achievement levels

Content and communication		
Level 3	Level 2	Level 1
		✓

Student 1's response contains some relevant words, but in places he moves away from the image and spends too long on details of his previous visit. There are also some places where his communication is not clear.

- We can't be sure it is cold, as there is no evidence of that.
- What does he mean by 'conkreet'? We have to work that out.
- He tells us that the park has 'few trees'. But, as you can see, the park is full of trees.

Language		
Level 3	Level 2	Level 1
		✓

We are concentrating on Student 1's spelling and punctuation – he can have some errors in his grammar so we will not worry about that. Student 1's use of simple words is reasonable and he spells some of them correctly. He doesn't use full stops or appropriate punctuation.

- Student 1 hasn't spelt the two more complex words, 'concrete' and 'beautiful', correctly, and he has made mistakes in the spelling of some simple words (picture, inside, between).
- Student 1 hasn't used commas correctly or the necessary full stops to make complete sentences.
- Student 1 has not used capital letters where necessary.

Examples of mistakes to avoid:

✗ 'In the pictare is park' – Student 1 has missed out the article. Either 'a' or 'the' between 'is' and 'park' would work but 'is park' is not as clear as it could be.

✗ 'it look like' – This should be 'it looks like', so Student 1 has not made the verb agree with the subject. However, he will not lose marks as his grammar is not being assessed.

✗ 'beatifull' – This word is not spelled correctly – it should be 'beautiful'. Student 1 will lose marks for spelling that is not accurate.

Sample response – Student 2

> The photograph shows a bright and sunny view of a large park in the centre of a city. The park, which contains at least two lakes, is lined by buildings, and skirting these is a wide river that flows out to the sea beyond. There are some extremely tall skyscrapers.

Examiner Feedback

Achievement levels

Content and communication		
Level 3	Level 2	Level 1
✓		

This response is entirely relevant and Student 2 has conveyed a description of the photograph with full clarity.

- Student 2 has used exactly 50 words and this is ideal.
- She has captured the moment and shows this in her opening sentence.
- The focus on the relationship between nature (park, river, sea) and humans (buildings, skyscrapers) is well done.
- She returns to the idea of the city, finishing with the front of the picture – the skyscrapers.

Language		
Level 3	Level 2	Level 1
✓		

Student 2 uses very proficient language, and although she is assessed only for spelling and punctuation, there are areas of her writing that are strong.

- Student 2 uses simple but effective adjectives, spelled correctly, which describe the weather and the view.
- She focuses on a specific aspect – the lakes in the park – and uses 'at least' appropriately to cover the possibility of more lakes we can't see.
- In describing the lakes, she uses a well-controlled subordinate clause.
- She is in control of her sentences, with a longer complex sentence coming just before the final short sentence.
- She uses the complex words 'lined' and 'skirting' to good effect.

Sample response – Student 3

> I see this from very tall viewpoint so I can also see other tall bildings surrounding the park. The main thing I saw is the park, and its a very green one with looking like two lake. Hey, what a very plesant day it is and the distance river is shinning nice. Mostly – sitting in the middle of the city I observe the water and nature.

Examiner Feedback

Achievement levels

Content and communication		
Level 3	Level 2	Level 1
	✓	

This response has content that is mostly relevant. Student 3 has communicated this reasonably well, but we do have to pause at times when reading it.

- Student 3 has gone over the suggested word limit by 16 words. She has used 66 words. In this case, her last sentence continues her content and communication skills.
- Student 3's first two sentences would work better if they were reversed.
- Student 3 chooses an informal way to communicate the sunny outlook, but this is at odds with the rest of her writing.

Language		
Level 3	Level 2	Level 1
	✓	

This response uses some complex words, the spelling is mostly accurate, and some of the sentences are controlled with punctuation – but there are places where the language is not correct.

- In going over the top limit of 50 words, Student 3 risks making some errors in her language. However, her last sentence has no errors in terms of spelling or punctuation.
- It's good to see the use of more complex words such as 'viewpoint' and 'observe'. 'Pleasant' is not spelled correctly, but this is a minor slip. Student 3 also meant to use 'distant' rather than 'distance', but this is a complex word and she made a good attempt at spelling it.
- 'Surrounding' is a good verb, and it is spelled correctly.
- Student 3's use of sentences is generally good. Only her last sentence is confusing – and that is because the phrase 'sitting in the middle of the city' works as a fronted adverbial. Try adding the phrase at the end.

Examples of mistakes to avoid:

✗ 'I see this from very tall viewpoint' – The article is missing between 'from' and 'tall'. It needs an 'a' to be accurate (from a very). In English there are two types of article: definite (the) and indefinite (a, an). Including an article increases fluency in your writing and speaking, but doesn't usually have a big effect on meaning.

✗ 'its a very green one' – Student 3 has tried to use the contraction for 'it is' but has forgotten the apostrophe (it's). This is a very common error, but easy to correct.

✗ 'Hey, what a very' – It's not a good idea to mix different styles of writing in Task 1. Student 3 has tried to be informal with this phrase, but the description needs a more formal style. Check that your style stays consistent.

Task 1

Our model answers show you how to approach the task, providing appropriate content using language that is correct. They are not designed to be responses that gain full marks – in other words, some students will be able to provide stronger and better responses. However, the model answer will help you to stay on track and hopefully help you do the best you can.

Model answer to Task 1

> The photo is taken from a high place, with a view of tall buildings and a large green park in the middle of a city. I can also see water – two lakes, a river, and the sea beyond. It's a bright, sunny day. Green and white show a pleasant contrast.

Revision Tip

Use the 'Common scenes' section on page 102 and the photograph in question 01, and search the internet for similar photographs of landscapes and city scenes. Look for photos that have something in the centre (or something that catches your eye in the front) as well as views behind and beyond. Then practise writing 30–50 words describing what you see from both aspects (front/centre + distance/behind). There is no need to rush. Think about only what you see and what is factual. Don't add descriptions of what is not actually there. Once you have written about ten of these types of descriptions, you should be ready and prepared!

How well did you do on Task 1?

Use the levels given to Students 1, 2, and 3, and look back at your response to the task to see where it fits best. This is your achievement level (examiners call this a band).

Examiner Input

An examiner will use the following approach in marking your writing for all four tasks:

- They will start at the lowest level of their mark scheme and use it like a ladder to see how far you can climb.
- When they find a match between your writing level and the words that describe that level they will stop – as that is your achievement level.
- To get to the level, they will look at the overall quality of your written response. In other words, they do not try to find every single mistake in your writing – they use what we call a 'best fit' approach.
- In cases where there are 2 or 3 marks available in a level (for example 6–7 or 13–15), the examiner considers how close your work is to the top of the level or the lower part of the level. That is how they choose the final mark.
- Examiners will refer to sample answers from other students who have taken the examination.

My levels for Task 1	Content and communication: Level _____
	Language: Level _____
What I found difficult	
What I have learnt	
Three ways I can improve	• _____
	• _____
	• _____

If you would like a numerical score, use the grid below to decide on a mark depending on whether you feel your writing is stronger than the sample student answers, or perhaps not quite as good.

My mark for Task 1			
Content and communication	**My mark**	**Language**	**My mark**
Level 3 (5 or 6 marks)		Level 3 (3 marks)	
Level 2 (3 or 4 marks)		Level 2 (2 marks)	
Level 1 (1 or 2 marks)		Level 1 (1 mark)	
Total of the two marks for Task 1			_____ / 9

Task 2

Now let's move on to Task 2 on the Writing paper, where you are asked to write a letter.

Common letters

Letter-writing topics that have appeared in previous exams include:

- a letter to school parents inviting them to a charity music concert at the school – persuading them to attend

- a letter to a friend informing them about voluntary work you are doing – persuading them to assist you

- a letter to a friend inviting them to a family celebration – persuading them why they should come

- a letter to a family member explaining how they can become healthier and fitter – informing them how you can help them

- a letter to the members of a sports club informing them about the end-of-year awards evening – explaining why they should attend.

What do we notice about Task 2?

For Task 2, we know that:

- it's always a letter

- commonly used purposes for the writing are to **invite**, **inform**, **explain**, and **persuade**

- your audience or reader is specified.

In other words, you know who you are writing to and why. You will need to use some formal language even if you are writing to a friend. If you are writing to people you don't know, you can use friendly language, but not casual language.

What are the key assessment elements of Task 2?

Marks available	Number of words to write	How I will gain marks
12 marks – 1 task	50–70 words	- by producing clear and coherent text of extended length to present key points, details and ideas (W2) - by making accurate use of vocabulary and grammar, and by spelling and punctuating accurately (W3)

Key Points

In Task 2, you are asked to write a letter that has two main purposes – for example, to inform the reader about something that is going to happen soon, and to then persuade them to do it.

The persuade part is often shown by using 'why' in one of the three bullet points. There will always be three bullet points and you must use them – in other words, they are compulsory and not optional.

You need to respond to each bullet point and you can do this one-by-one from the first one to the third one, ideally using two or three paragraphs. You can also respond to the bullet points in the order you prefer.

You are provided with about 20 answer lines to write your letter – this is plenty and you should not need to write outside the page. As with Task 1, try to stay within the word count as this is your best chance of doing well.

Examiner Input

You should aim for between 50 and 70 words, as longer responses could impact on quality if you begin to stray from the main three bullet points or if you write too much. Remember, in Task 2, you must use the bullet points – they are compulsory. If you do end up with more than 70 words, the examiner will still mark your whole response and you will not be penalised unless your content, communication, or language weakens.

Assessment Objectives

W2 and W3. For Task 2 you can achieve highly by writing only 50 words. Remember that (unlike Task 1) you will be assessed on all four parts of W3: vocabulary, grammar, punctuation, and spelling. W2 focuses on how well you show the key points of your letter – that is, how well you provide the details and ideas to communicate your message to the audience/reader(s), and how you use a variety of vocabulary and structures.

Now let's explore an example of Task 2 and the style of writing you need to practise. Read question 02 on page 112 and the guidance here and at the top of page 113, and then respond to the task.

Exam Tip

In Task 2, you are more likely to be responding to the topics that occur in all three themes. For example, charity/voluntary work (Theme two, Topic 2), life at school (Theme three, Topic 2), family celebrations (Theme one, Topic 1), and sport (Theme one, Topic 3) have all been used. The important thing to note is that the topic is given to you in the opening lines on the examination paper. If you link the topic to the theme it may help trigger some useful content that you can focus on from your lessons and schoolwork. So, if your topic is a family celebration, think about the theme of identity and culture, and what you could write about.

Exam-style questions

02 You are planning a walk around your local town.

Write a letter to a friend inviting them to complete the walk with you.

You **must** write about:

- **where** the walk will go in the town
- **what** the purpose of your walk is
- **why** your friend should join you.

Your letter should be between 50 and 70 words. Do **not** write an address.   **[12 marks]**

_____

_____

_____

_____

_____

_____

_____

_____

_____

_____

_____

_____

_____

_____

_____

_____

Language Support

- You are writing a **letter**, so it is best to use the accepted opening style of 'Dear …' and a suitable way to close the letter, such as 'Many thanks', but ideally change this to suit the purpose and style of the letter. For this letter, you could use:

  Dear Amie,

  I'm going on an organised walk soon …

  Hope to see you there,

  Fay

- You can use the **voice** of someone else rather than yourself in the letter. For example, you could pretend that you are one of the organisers of the walk if you feel it would be easier. However, think about how it affects the language you will use. For example, an organiser may use more formal language to describe the walk, but remember that this task is to write to a friend, so it should not be too formal. For example: 'We have organised this walk to promote the work of our tourist centre …'. Notice also how you will need to use different pronouns.

- Aim for at least one **compound** or **complex sentence** to justify the 'why' element of Task 2 – usually, why someone should attend or be involved. For example, 'You will get some fresh air <u>and</u> meet new people' is good as a compound sentence, but better and more complex is 'Meet new friends, in fresh air, to have a great day out' because it includes a subordinate clause.

- When you are writing longer pieces, think about using an **association chain** – each new word in the chain forming a connection with the one before. For example, this chain could work well for Task 2: town – walk – organised – highlights – benefits – funds – charity.

 Exam Tip

Try to write in a semi-formal style. You can use informal methods such as abbreviations and idioms. For example, '<u>I'm</u> going on the walk and I <u>can't</u> wait to start', along with the idiom 'It'll be <u>a walk down memory lane</u> for me and you'. But try to blend these with more formal language where appropriate. For example, 'It is an official, organised walk' and 'It is thought that thousands will attend'. So a full version with semi-formal language might be:

Dear Gianni

Next week we can go on a walk down memory lane if you like. I'm going, and I can't wait to start. It is an official, organised walk and it is thought that thousands might attend …

Examiner feedback and raising my grade

Now that you have written your response to Task 2, look at the three sample responses to the same task, and the guidance, tips, and advice offered.

Achievement levels

We are using the same method to mark each sample response as we did for Task 1 and that follows the way an examiner will assess your writing. Here is a reminder of the two criteria that apply to all of the Writing paper tasks:

- **Content and communication:** You can think of this as how clearly you have conveyed the content you have chosen to write about to your reader.

- **Language:** This is your accurate and appropriate use of language. It also includes your variety of words, phrases, punctuation, sentences, and structures.

For Task 2, there are four levels available for each criterion – Level 3 is the best/highest and Level 0 means that a response doesn't have enough merit to be awarded any marks at all. Here, let's focus on working at Levels 3, 2, and 1.

Task 2

Sample answers to Task 2
Sample response – Student 1

Dear Sally,

Next week I will going on an walk in our town. I'm doing the walk for charity for children. People who finish the walk get a voucha and the vouchure use to buy us a book or CD and the money then go to the charity.

Do you know the old clock building in town. We will begin there and we walked along park to the river area crossing the bridge to the musseem. After that, we seeing the volley balling place are other friends like to play.

Sally come please as you will get healthy than before and you can meat people and you can make money.

Let me know,

Jonas

Examiner Feedback

Achievement levels

Content and communication		
Level 3	Level 2	Level 1
	✓	

This response from Student 1 is mostly relevant.

- The first sentence in the second paragraph is a question, but it doesn't have a question mark.
- Student 1 uses three paragraphs and this shows some understanding of how to separate different ideas and points. However, this has taken him over the upper word limit (70) to 107 words. We know that the examiner will read all the words for all the tasks, so this allows Student 1 to stay in Level 2 as his extra words are still relevant and his language level stays about the same.

Language		
Level 3	Level 2	Level 1
	✓	

As you will see from mistakes made by Student 1, he can use some complex words and spell them correctly, but he makes several errors throughout his letter.

- He was not able to spell the two more complex words 'voucher' and 'museum' correctly.
- His verb tenses are not accurate – he mixes up past, present, and future. However, we can follow his sentences and this means he has some successful use of grammar and structures.
- We notice that he spells meet as 'meat', which is a homophone. However, this is a slip and his other simpler words are spelled correctly.

Examples of mistakes to avoid:

✗ 'I will going' – The addition of 'be' is needed to use the future action properly – will + be + the present participle (the root verb + -ing). The simple future is a verb tense that is used when an action is expected to occur in the future and be completed.

✗ 'voucha and the vouchure' – Student 1 attempts to spell the word 'voucher' phonetically. This is fine and he gets quite close. However, when trying this, be consistent with the spelling and do not use more than one attempt if you don't actually know how to spell the word. Remember that all of the tasks in the Writing paper test your spelling.

✗ 'We will begin there and we walked' – Avoid mixing up verb tenses. Here, the future and the past tense are used close to each other, and it's confusing, resulting in problems with communication.

✗ 'we seeing the volley balling place are other friends like to play' – Here, 'are' should be 'our'. Be careful with 'are' and 'our'. They can be pronounced similarly in English (homophones), but they have very different meanings. 'Are' is the second person singular present and the first, second, and third person plural present of the verb 'to be'. 'Our' is a determiner belonging to or associated with the speaker and one or more other people previously mentioned.

✗ 'and you can meat people and you' – Try not to use the conjunction 'and' more than once in a shorter sentence. This is sometimes called a 'run-on sentence' and can usually be avoided. For example, 'and you can meet people but also make money' is better use of English.

Sample response – Student 2

I would like to get you to my walk wich is going as a run on next week under Town. It my new idea. All town people; enjoy this occasion, first of us as will see the volley ball. Main reason we do is to fit keep and to make new walkers come you should come to be happy.

Examiner Feedback

Achievement levels

Content and communication		
Level 3	Level 2	Level 1
		✓

Student 2 responds in a minimal way to the bullet points, but there are some relevant words and phrases that relate to the main purpose of the letter.

- There is a walk and it is happening in the town.
- However, Student 2's friend is likely to think that the walk is Student 2's idea and it's her walk, not an organised walk. It should be treated as her own walk because the task requires it to be hers.
- It's not clear what the occasion is – why would the people of the town enjoy it?

- Student 2 responds to the second bullet point (purpose) by mentioning that they will see volley ball on the route – but this is only one clue.
- Student 2 does say why her friend should go but in her first reason, the order of the words 'fit keep' is wrong, and should be 'keep fit'. The second reason is confusing – to 'make new walkers'? The wrong word here changes the meaning and blurs the communication.

Language		
Level 3	Level 2	Level 1
		✓

Student 2's language is simple and her simple words are generally spelled correctly. She also uses some simple punctuation appropriately. However, her grammar is limited and her letter has a lot of errors.

- Student 2 confuses us with a walk that is going 'as a run'. Student 2 means the walk is going to run next week. However, her choice of vocabulary is not appropriate here.
- Using the preposition 'under' is not appropriate with the word town in this context.
- Student 2's limited grammar shows as she struggles to separate out the sentences. The final sentence has two reasons, not one, and the implication is that her friend should come to make new walkers come.

Examples of mistakes to avoid:

✗ 'wich is going' – Look at the spelling of 'which'. It's important to learn and practise the spelling of the 'wh' words as getting these wrong can affect the flow (fluency) of your writing and will be noticed quickly by your reader(s). All of these are common 'wh' words: which, why, where, who, what, whether, when, whose, whilst.

✗ 'All town people; enjoy this occasion' – The use of the semicolon (;) is not correct here. Be careful when you use it and don't try to use it because you think you should. The sentence doesn't need punctuation in these first six words.

✗ 'to make new walkers' – Here, Student 2 wants to use 'meet' but has used 'make'. You can usually spot this kind of error (a wrong choice of words) when you quickly check your writing. Look out for words that don't seem to fit.

Sample response – Student 3

> Dear Gianni
>
> Have you heard about the organise walk? It's a new one and it's to promote the old part of town to tourism. Our town is so historic and we have interesting places to exhibit, such as the museum of local art and the ancient history museum.
>
> Please join me as we can exercise, explore places we have not been to, and bolster the town's tourist centre. They will give us a T-shirt; 'Town Walkers 2022' on the back!
>
> Romany

Examiner Feedback

Achievement levels

Content and communication		
Level 3	Level 2	Level 1
✓		

This response from Student 3 has fully relevant details that communicate all the bullet points clearly.

- The purpose of the walk is dealt with quickly, and with supporting detail.

- The response to 'where' is integrated with the purpose and this is very efficient use of content to communicate.

- Three reasons are given by Student 3 to answer the 'why' prompt and they are all highly relevant to the task. However, had he provided one appropriate reason this would be fine.

- The add-on of the free T-shirt is a nice touch even though it takes Student 3 slightly over the word count at 78 words. This will not make any difference to the mark that the examiner awards.

Language		
Level 3	Level 2	Level 1
✓		

Almost all the spelling is accurate, and punctuation is a strong point for Student 3. There is a variety of structures and a range of vocabulary confirms top-level writing.

- A rhetorical question opens the piece of writing to good effect.

- The slight error – organise walk, rather than organised – is very minor and will not affect the overall mark as examiners will always look to reward the writing as a whole and not 'pick holes' in a response.

- The use of 'exhibit' and 'bolster' (bolster means support and strengthen) demonstrates sophisticated vocabulary.

- 'such as' is a better way to give examples than using 'like'.

- The triplet – the use of three clauses in a sentence – is very effective in the second paragraph.

- The use of the colon after T-shirt is also correct as is the use of the inverted commas. It's also a strong way to end the letter.

Examples of mistakes to avoid:

✗ 'promote the old part of town to tourism' – Here, 'to' is not the right preposition, but it is close and the meaning is not affected. Student 3 means 'promote … for tourism' or she could have said 'promote … to tourists'. Try to learn prepositions that are normally used with other words. Some examples beginning with 'b' associated with a house: below the roof, behind the curtain, beneath this floor, and between the two cabinets.

✗ 'Our town is so historic' – Be careful with the word 'so' and try not to use it too much. Student 3 uses it to emphasise the age of the town, but it would be better to use another word such as 'very', 'extremely' or, even better, 'impressively'. You can use 'so' as a coordinating conjunction, for example: 'The town has ancient buildings, so let's go and explore them.'

Task 2

Revision Tip

For a piece of extended writing, it's always a good idea to spend some time thinking about a plan. You will have time in the examination and this time is better spent on a brief plan rather than writing over the suggested top end limit for words. An example of a detailed plan for Task 2 is below, but in the actual exam you will not have time to write detailed notes like these.

- Need a reason for why the walk is taking place – only need to give one reason
- It's a letter to a friend, so I use standard letter form with 'Dear Alan' and 'See you soon' at end
- In our town – so think of two/three places I know well
- Be good to have another separate reason why friend should come – exercise? Learn about town they don't know? Meet new people?

You can practise this approach by thinking of similar letters that have a specified audience, and then making brief notes for the plan. But don't spend more than 3 or 4 minutes on the plans! Here is an example for you:

> Your school or college is holding a fun run.
> Write a letter to parents inviting them to join in on the run.
>
> Purpose:
>
> I'll say that the reason is to raise money for a local charity – maybe for a children's hospital?
>
> Audience/reader(s):
>
> Parents, but perhaps they can bring other members of family and friends. I'll mention that.
>
> Details/points to convey:
>
> Price of ticket. Route of the run. Can also be walked, no pressure, it's fun! Maybe mention we will run around the lake?
>
> The 'why' part – Task 2 always has a 'why should he/she/they get involved?':
>
> I can include good exercise, fresh air, meet new people, feel-good factor to donate money, involve with school …. But better I stick to 2 good reasons as I only have 70 words.

Try writing the letter in the space below yourself and don't go over 80 words! And then have a look at our model answer on the next page.

_____

_____

_____

_____

_____

_____

_____

_____

_____

_____

_____

_____

_____

_____

_____

_____

_____

_____

_____

_____

_____

_____

_____

_____

_____

_____

Model answer to Task 2

This model answer is based on the revision tip on the previous page.

> Dear parents
>
> Our school is holding a fun run to raise money for the children's hospital in town. You are invited to join in and please bring along other members of your family and some friends. You don't need to run – you can walk the route!
>
> The ticket costs £10. Our route includes a lovely lakeside view of the tall evergreen trees. It's a great chance to get some fresh air and support the school community.
>
> Many thanks
>
> Student Council

Task 2

How well did you do on Task 2?

Use the levels given to Students 1, 2, and 3, and look back at your response to the task to see where it fits best. This is your probable/likely achievement level (examiners call this a band).

My levels for Task 2	Content and communication: Level _____ Language: Level _____
What I found difficult	
What I have learnt	
Three ways I can improve	• _____ • _____ • _____

If you would like a numerical score, use the grid below to decide on a mark depending on whether you feel your writing is stronger than the sample student answers, or perhaps not quite as good as theirs.

My mark for Task 2			
Content and communication	**My mark**	**Language**	**My mark**
Level 3 (5 or 6 marks)		Level 3 (5 or 6 marks)	
Level 2 (3 or 4 marks)		Level 2 (3 or 4 marks)	
Level 1 (1 or 2 marks)		Level 1 (1 or 2 marks)	
Total of the two marks for Task 2			_____ / 12

Task 3

Now let's look closely at Task 3, where the form of the writing may vary. For example, you might be asked to write an article, email, blog, or report.

Common formats

Extended writing tasks that have appeared in previous exams include:

- an email to a friend about a careers event you attended with your school – including your opinion of the event

- an article for a local newspaper about a recent special event at your school – and what you felt about it

- an article for your school magazine about a lesson you enjoy – explaining why you enjoy it

- a blog about a film you saw that you enjoyed – and why you liked the film

- a blog about your post-school/college plans for the next two years – including your plans for a career, explaining your reasons.

What do we notice about Task 3?

As you can see, Task 3 uses a range of formats, which can affect the style of writing you produce. An email is not quite the same as a blog, and an article differs from a report. However, don't worry about getting the format perfected – it is the quality of your writing and the content you provide that is important.

In Task 3, you are combining two styles of writing:

- writing to inform/explain + writing to convey feelings/opinions.

What are the key assessment elements of Task 3?

Marks available	Number of words to write	How I will gain marks
16 marks – 1 task	70–90 words	• by producing a clear and coherent text of extended length to present key points, details and ideas (W2) • by making accurate use of vocabulary and grammatical structures; by spelling and punctuating accurately (W3) • by manipulating language with increasing fluency and creativity for a variety of purposes (W4)

Key Points

In Task 3, you are asked to write a response that has two main purposes: **to inform** the reader about something that you have probably already done, seen, or attended, and then **to convey** your feelings and opinions about it. However, the event could also be imagined and a future event. The second part is usually indicated by phrases such as: 'your opinion', 'your feelings', 'why you liked/enjoyed it'.

You are likely to be asked about something from the past, but check the question's wording carefully, as you may be able to focus on the present. For example, a lesson you enjoy can be expressed using the past and the present tenses. If future action is required, the task will clearly signpost this (for example, any career plans you have once you leave school).

Usually, there are three or four bullet points. As with Task 2, they are compulsory, so you must respond to all four. You are usually required to provide details for the first three bullet points, and convey some feelings, opinions, and possibly a justification to respond to the fourth bullet point. We recommend that you respond to the bullet points in order, completing your writing by responding to the fourth or final prompt, ideally with a separate paragraph.

You are provided with about 20 answer lines to write your letter – this is plenty, and you should not need to write outside the page. As with Tasks 1 and 2, try to stay within the word count as this is your best chance of doing well.

Exam Tip

In Task 3, Theme three often features. For example, responding to the topics such as your studies, life at school/college, education post-16, jobs, career choices, and ambitions. However, you might be asked to write about something from Themes one or two – for example, a film you saw and liked. In this unit, we will focus on helping you prepare for a Theme three topic.

Assessment Objectives

W2, W3 and W4. Task 3 is 70–90 words, so is a more extended piece of writing. In W3, as in Task 2, you are assessed on all four parts: vocabulary, grammar, punctuation, and spelling. W2 focuses on how well you provide the details that relate to the first prompts and communicate these to your audience/reader(s).

Task 3 introduces a new assessment criterion, W4, and this is how you will gain higher marks. The examiner will be looking at how well you have controlled your language and manipulated it (whether you have handled it with skill) to match the specific purpose and audience. Hopefully, you can produce some creative and flowing (fluent) writing, and practising here and in the next unit should help you to achieve it.

Examiner Input

You should aim for between 70 and 90 words because responses that are too long might result in losing balance across the required bullet-point prompts. If you do end up with more than 90 words, the examiner will still mark your whole response and you will not be penalised. However, in Task 3, missing a prompt will certainly result in a lower mark as your coverage of detail will be lower. Also take care to give enough time and space to cover the final bullet point, as too many students skim over this. Providing a full response to this point will give you a better chance of securing a higher mark.

Exam-style questions

Now let's explore an example of Task 3 and the style of writing you need to practise. Read question 03 on page 123 and the guidance on pages 122 and 125, and then respond to the task.

03 Write a blog about a part-time job you have been doing in the last few months.

You **must** write about:

- **what** the job is
- **where** you do it
- **who** you work with
- **why** you enjoy your part-time job.

Your blog should be between 70 and 90 words.

[16 marks]

_____

_____

_____

_____

_____

_____

_____

_____

_____

_____

_____

_____

_____

_____

_____

_____

Language Support

1 If you are writing a **blog**, focus on these three aspects of blog writing:

- Keep your reader interested until the end, as blogs should have a strong sense of audience.

- Remember a blog is writing for sharing and not writing that is just for yourself (so it's not a personal diary).

- Convey your feelings or opinions, as a blog builds on the input of others over time. Think of a blog as a diary for many people to read. A blog is not quite as formal as an article – you can be slightly less formal in a blog, but should be slightly more formal in an article.

2 Be careful not to overuse **idioms**, as this can sound awkward. Idioms are a feature of the English language, and speakers and writers of English use them a lot. However, if idioms are used out of context, they can compromise your meaning and reduce your marks. For example, there are many idioms associated with working, and here is one that fits well to the context of Task 3: 'My father said I'm working for peanuts, but I told him it's not the money, it's the experience I want.' However, many idioms about 'work' would not be appropriate in this Task 3 context, so if you are planning to use an idiom be sure that you completely understand its meaning.

3 Because you have to use all the bullet points in Task 3, we recommend that you use them to structure your **paragraphing**. As you can see in the model answer for Task 3 (page 132), you can certainly use two paragraphs. Using three paragraphs would also be fine. If you are given four bullet points, a good approach is to combine the details of bullet points 1 and 2 into one paragraph, have a new paragraph for point 3, and then a concluding paragraph for point 4. Combining points 3 and 4 into a single paragraph will also usually work.

4 In Tasks 3 and 4, you can demonstrate your variety of **vocabulary**, **structures,** and also **tenses** if you feel comfortable to do so, although staying in the same tense is acceptable. We recommend that you have a method to check that you are developing your range. For example, the word AVOCADO can help to remember to use a range of: adjectives, verbs, connectives, and adverbs to help gain marks for vocabulary. In Tasks 3 and 4, opinions and originality are rewarded (the two Os from AVOCADO) but you don't need to come up with anything original. You can still do well if you explain things clearly and accurately. The D is for description and in Tasks 3 and 4 you can think of this as varying the way in which you provide information and supporting details.

5 Remember to use two or three good, **complex sentences** that contain **subordinate clauses** to add details. Compound sentences are good also, but always see if you can remove the conjunction and make a more sophisticated sentence. An example for Task 3 is changing 'I work at a supermarket and I fill shelves in a team' to the much better, and complex sentence, 'I work at a supermarket, as part of a lively and funny team, where I fill shelves.' We have removed the conjunction (and) and used an adverb (where). This allows us to include a subordinating clause with commas.

Exam Tip

It's not a good idea to pre-learn phrases that you then insert into your responses. Let's have a look at an example for Task 3 which is about working part-time. You may have learnt the phrase 'the extra income certainly helps', but if, for example, you are writing about a part-time job where you volunteer, this phrase would not be appropriate as you are not getting paid for your work. Pre-learning a lot of phrases is never a good idea. However, using your own knowledge of a topic is useful in Tasks 2, 3, and 4 of the Writing paper, as it will help you provide details.

Examiner feedback and raising my grade

Now that you have written your response to Task 3, look at the four sample responses below, and the guidance, tips, and advice offered.

Achievement levels

Here is a reminder of the two criteria that apply to all of the Writing paper tasks:

- **Content and communication**: This is how clearly you have conveyed the content you have chosen to write about to your reader.
- **Language**: This is the accurate, appropriate, and varied use of words, phrases, punctuation, sentences, and structures.

For Task 3, there are five levels available for each criterion, so this is one more than for Tasks 1 and 2. Level 4 is the best/highest and Level 0 means that a response doesn't have enough merit to be awarded any marks at all. Here, let's focus on working at Levels 4, 3, 2, and 1.

Sample answers to Task 3

Sample response – Student 1

> For last few weeks I has been saleing in a shop as assisent for sale. I do this work in a sale shop near to college so I is not far to walk after class. I do it in the sale team and I do sale every week on Wendesday and Saturday. Not on another time. One time was when we sale none and the manager was happy.
>
> I enjoy cos it gives me a change and meeting. All the time meeting.

 Examiner Feedback

Achievement levels

Content and communication			
Level 4	Level 3	Level 2	Level 1
		✓	

This response from Student 1 is satisfactory and is generally relevant. Student 1 has responded to all of the bullet points, but there are moments where her communication breaks down.

- Responding to the third bullet point – the memorable occasion – Student 1's message is confusing. Why would the sales manager be happy if nothing was sold?
- Student 1's explanation of why she enjoys the job is not clear. Does she mean she enjoys meeting people or going to meetings whilst at work?
- Student 1 has written 82 words for her blog.

Language			
Level 4	Level 3	Level 2	Level 1
		✓	

Student 1's spelling and punctuation overall is accurate more often than her errors. There is an attempt at some variation of words used. However:

- selling, assistant, and Wednesday are not spelled correctly
- she uses the word 'sale' five times – she could have varied this by using synonyms or alternative words (for example, instead of a 'sale shop' she could have told the reader what type of shop it is)
- Student 1 would have benefited from using more words associated with working in sales and in shops
- her control of verbs and tenses is variable, but she does have some correct usage – for example, 'I enjoy cos it gives me a change …'.

Examples of mistakes to avoid:

✗ 'I has been saleing' – 'has been' is used with singular nouns in the third person and 'have been' is used in first/second person singular and all plural cases. So, this should be 'I have been'. The present participle of the verb 'to sell' is 'selling'.

✗ 'so I is not far' – The correct pronoun to use here is 'it', not 'I'. However, we do know what Student 1 means, so this error does not affect the meaning of the sentence.

✗ 'I do sale' – Student 1 has used two verbs here where only one is needed. There is no need to use the verb 'to do' before another verb, unless you are using 'do' to give emphasis to another verb. For example, 'I do want to be the best salesperson this month.' Student 1 means that she sells on two days a week and should have written 'I sell every week …'.

✗ 'cos' – Avoid using 'cos' as a short form of 'because'. This can be effective if you are using dialogue but in formal and semi-formal language it's regarded as slang.

Sample response – Student 2

Let me tell you about my own part-time working. Since a few months I have been helping my father in his company which is a company making medical gear. I am lucky as the place to work is my father's place so I can go with him. I only work on Tuesdays, my day off from college. One time, we arrived in a storm, and my farther made me clean the car!

I appresiate that as I plan to be a doctor, and it gives me some medical experients.

Examiner Feedback

Achievement levels

Content and communication			
Level 4	Level 3	Level 2	Level 1
	✓		

This response from Student 2 is good, and mostly relevant. He has responded well to all of the bullet points, but unfortunately the last sentence is a bit puzzling.

- He starts well with his use of 'Let me tell you about …' – a useful semi-formal blog-style opener.
- Student 2 uses up several lines in responding to what the job is and where it is done – he could have been more efficient and used fewer words. However, his writing is still good.
- He reports his memorable occasion well and with a sense of humour.
- Student 2 has written 89 words for his blog.

Language			
Level 4	Level 3	Level 2	Level 1
	✓		

Student 2's spelling and punctuation are generally accurate, but with a few slight errors. These slips are minor and do not affect the fluency of reading the blog. His grammar is sound and he varies his vocabulary.

- Student 2 has spelled 'appreciate' and 'experience' wrong, but these are more challenging words to spell. He also slips with the second spelling of father, adding an 'r' (which changes the meaning of the word in English) and which the examiner will notice!
- There should not be a comma after 'storm' as this is not a subordinating clause, but this is a minor grammatical error.
- The relation between pronouns and their antecedents is unclear at times.

Examples of mistakes to avoid:

✗ 'Since a few months' – 'Since' can be used as a preposition, a conjunction, and an adverb. Student 2 is using it as a preposition, but it would have been better if Student 2 had used the word 'for'.

✗ 'medical gear' – Using 'gear' in this context is too informal. A better word is 'equipment'. However, 'My dad makes sure I take the right gear to work' would be an appropriate use in the context, as this is a less formal sentence.

✗ 'it gives' – Look back to the previous sentences to trace the pronoun 'it'. What does it refer to? Does it refer to the determiner 'that'? If so, what does 'that' refer back to? It looks like the cleaning of the car. Can you see the confusion? Examiners refer to this as ambiguous language.

Sample response – Student 3

I luckey as job is homework. I do is put item in a bocks. I do this from house. My mom doesnt she she not mind it. Sometime bock is larg one time like I put item in boxx and to heavy too move I stop like if I want having a juse I like a food as job is me and my mom say eating and work is too watch.

Examiner Feedback

Achievement levels

Content and communication			
Level 4	Level 3	Level 2	Level 1
			✓

This is a limited response, but not in the number of words. Student 3 attempts the task and gives some relevant information, but he doesn't address the final prompt about why he enjoys his part-time work. Student 3's communication breaks down frequently, too.

- We have to infer that his job is not homework set by his school, but a job he does at home. He does clear this up however in his third sentence.
- We are not sure if Student 3's mother approves of his work at home job due to the double negatives used ('doesn't', 'not').
- When Student 3 says 'job is me' we have to infer again what he means – we think he means that how he does his job is 'up to him'.
- What does Student 3 mean when he says that his mom says that eating and working is 'to watch'? He could mean his 'mom' thinks it's too much. But he could also mean that his mother is telling him to watch what he is doing as it's not sensible.
- Student 3 has written 71 words for his blog and this is inside the suggested amount.

Language			
Level 4	Level 3	Level 2	Level 1
			✓

Student 3 has frequent errors in spelling and punctuation, and these affect how fluently the reader can read the blog. There are issues with Student 3's grammar and structures.

- Student 3 has spelled 'lucky', 'box', 'large', and 'juice' wrong. These are higher frequency words, so it is important to spell them correctly to get above Level 1.
- Student 3 uses four simple sentences where he could have combined them by using conjunctions.
- This is followed by a very long and uncontrolled final sentence that has frequent structural errors.
- Student 3's writing needs more grammar and more appropriate structuring.

Examples of mistakes to avoid:

✗ 'one time <u>like</u> I put item/ I stop <u>like</u> if' – Avoid using the word 'like' in this way as it's slang, and usually a lazy way of avoiding a replacement word or phrase. Instead of his first use, 'for example' would be better. His second use is not necessary as no additional word is needed.

✗ 'and to heavy too move' – Remember not to confuse the words 'to', 'too' (and 'two'). Student 3 has done that here. The preposition 'to' refers to a place, direction, or position. The adverb 'too' means also, very, extremely, or additionally.

Task 3

Sample response – Student 4

> I saw the advert a few months ago and I thought it was a great opportunity. Working at the sports centre that I go swimming at – perfect. I help the instructors with classes for young children.
>
> Last week we had an actually entertaining afternoon. We had a synchronised swimming team in to do a demonstration; their moves in the water were excellent.
>
> The people I work with are always positive and helpful, and they support me to learn about teaching swimming – that's the main reason I enjoy this job.

Ⓠ Examiner Feedback

Achievement levels

Content and communication			
Level 4	Level 3	Level 2	Level 1
✓			

Student 4 has written an excellent blog entry that is fully relevant, very clear, and easy to read and follow.

- She sets the context nicely, as she is familiar with the place of employment. She covers bullet points 1 and 2 succinctly.
- Her recall of the memorable event is very effective as it uses imagery and we can visualise the synchronised swimmers.
- The way she ends the blog is impressive – by providing the details first and then a nice finish with the reason.
- Student 4 has written 89 words and has done well to achieve the top level by staying close to the suggested word limit.

Language			
Level 4	Level 3	Level 2	Level 1
✓			

Student 4's spelling and punctuation are accurate and her control of grammar and structure is highly effective.

- Her use of the dash before 'perfect' shows her command of punctuation, and she introduces tone in the first part, which is a strong skill. Try reading it out loud.
- There is an effective use of a semicolon in the middle paragraph.
- Another effective use of the dash in the final paragraph turns a compound sentence into a complex one.
- Short sentences are used for effect, making this a controlled piece of writing.

Examples of mistakes to avoid:

- ✗ 'had an actually entertaining afternoon' – Student 4 hasn't used 'actually' correctly. People use this word a lot in speech but be careful when using it in writing. We can write this sentence in ways where the word is effective. For example, 'Last week we had an entertaining week actually' – it achieves the same effect as an adverb.

Revision Tip

Even though you don't have time in the examination to do a full check of your work, you do have some time, and we recommend that you allow for a few minutes to scan your writing. This is useful to make sure you have produced your best response, especially in Tasks 3 and 4 where you have written longer responses.

We don't recommend that you revise your writing. What you write in the examination is not a first draft, so you should be aiming for a complete piece from the moment you write. We discussed having a brief plan in our revision tip for Task 2, and that also applies for Tasks 3 and 4.

Here is a method you could use to carry out a quick check. You will need to remember the letters of course because you can't take anything into the exam room. But you can write these down on your paper as long as you avoid the dotted lines for your responses. Try to remember as many as you can.

SP	Spelling	PU	Punctuation		
WW	Wrong word	MW	Missing word	WO	Word order
VT	Verb tense	VA	Verb agreement	PR	Preposition
LS	Longer sentence	NC	Not clear	NN	Not needed

Now try a revision exercise in using these checking codes. Read the response to Task 3 below and see if you can use all the codes above, but only use each code once. Underline the relevant word(s) and draw an arrow to the two letters from the above list.

Resently, I started a new job on a local farm. The farm is just inside the farm close of my house. My main task is feeding the morning; that is I really look forward to part.

One time it was dark and I couldn't see so I fell over in some smelly manure it was awful. My dad telling me to work my own clothes in the machine.

Why do I enjoy my job? I enjoy it because I like being outside. In the fields. Even in rain.

I are going to work more hours soon.

Task 3

Now check your answers against this model answer. This is not a test of how many you got right, but a way to help you develop your own system of doing a similar, quick check on your writing.

Model answer to revision tip

SP	*Resently* should be spelled 'Recently'.

WO	**I really look forward to part** – The better word order would be 'the part I really look forward to'.

PU	**in some smelly manure it was awful** – This needs some punctuation, ideally after the word 'manure'. A comma would work, but a semi-colon would be better. A dash could also be used. It depends how much this student wants to emphasise falling into the manure.

WW	**work my own clothes** – We can infer from 'in the machine' that the student means 'wash' not 'work'.

NN	**Why** *do* **I enjoy my job?** – This isn't an effective rhetorical question. A better one is: 'What makes this job so great?' However, the student could have saved some words and not had a rhetorical question here.

Resently, I started a new job on a local farm. The farm is just inside the farm close of my house. My main task is feeding the in morning; that is I really look forward to part.

One time it was dark and I couldn't see and I fell over in some smelly manure it was awful. My dad telling me to work my own clothes in the machine.

Why do I enjoy my job? I enjoy it because I like being outside. In the fields. Even in rain. I are going to work more hours soon.

NC	**The farm is just inside the farm** – Does this mean the farm is close to a farm near the house? It needs to be clearer.

PR	**of my house** – The preposition is wrong. It should be 'to'.

MW	**feeding the in morning** – It looks as if the word 'animals' is missing, but the student could also have been more specific and used, for example, cows, chickens, and so on.

VT	**dad telling me** – The student should have used the past tense, 'My dad told me …'.

VA	**I are going** – The subject (I) and the verb (to be) are conjugated here as 'I am'.

LS	**I like being outside. In the fields. Even in rain.** – This can easily be made into a longer sentence. For example, 'I like being outside in the fields, even when it's raining.'

Model answer to Task 3

It's me again and guess what? I started a part-time job a few months ago. I work with my friend, Alice, and we operate a telephone information call line. We do this from an office in town. Tourists phone in and ask for information about the town.

Only last week, we had a call and the woman didn't say who she was until the end – turned out she was the Mayor! She said I did fine.

You know me, I love to talk and that's one reason I am enjoying the job. It's also helping me get through college as the money is quite good.

Note that this answer goes over the suggested word limit by 15 words. However, as the extra words remain relevant and do not have any errors, an examiner will read all of it and apply the mark scheme to it all. Therefore, you shouldn't worry if you do slip just over the word limit.

How well did you do on Task 3?

Use the levels given to the four students and look back at your response to the task to see where it fits best. This is your achievement level (examiners call this a band).

My levels for Task 3	Content and communication: Level _____ Language: Level _____
What I found difficult	_____ _____ _____
What I have learnt	_____ _____ _____
Four ways I can improve	• _____ • _____ • _____ • _____

If you would like a numerical score, use the grid below to decide on a mark depending on whether you feel your writing is stronger than the sample student answers, or perhaps not quite as good as theirs.

My mark for Task 3			
Content and communication	**My mark**	**Language**	**My mark**
Level 4 (7 or 8 marks)		Level 4 (7 or 8 marks)	
Level 3 (5 or 6 marks)		Level 3 (5 or 6 marks)	
Level 2 (3 or 4 marks)		Level 2 (3 or 4 marks)	
Level 1 (1 or 2 marks)		Level 1 (1 or 2 marks)	
Total of the two marks for Task 3			_____ / 16

Task 4

Task 4 is the final piece of writing required on the Writing paper. It's an extended piece and you are given a greater amount of flexibility in your choice of content and how you go about structuring your response. It's an opportunity to show what you can do and to demonstrate a good range of written skills.

Common prompts and topics

Extended writing tasks in previous exams have included:

- why we should protect the environment and how we can actually do this in practice – for your school magazine

- why it's important for young people to be healthy and how they can do this – for your school website

- why computers, tablets, and smartphones are helpful to students and how such digital devices can be used for learning

- why we all enjoy having friends, and how someone has been a good friend to you – for a blog

- a place you visited recently that impressed you and the reasons why you would like to go back there.

What do we notice about Task 4?

As you can see, Task 4 is much more about developing your own content within a specified but broad theme. You are sometimes given the format, such as an article, but your focus should be on combining two styles of writing: writing to inform/explain + writing a persuasive piece that can contain some opinions and possibly an argument for a case you are promoting and/or defending. You should assume an adult audience (such as your teacher or the examiner who will mark your writing).

What are the key assessment elements of Task 4?

Marks available	Number of words to write	How I will gain marks
23 marks – 1 task	100–150 words	<ul><li>by producing clear and coherent text of extended length to present key points, details and ideas (W2)</li><li>by making accurate use of vocabulary and grammar, and by spelling and punctuating accurately (W3)</li><li>by manipulating language with increasing fluency and creativity to match the purpose (W4)</li></ul>

Key Points

In Task 4, you are invited to write a longer piece than in the previous tasks – you have up to 150 words available. There is a dual purpose: to inform/explain, and also to persuade/argue. There are two bullet-point prompts only and these are optional – so you don't have to use them. However, we recommend that you do use them, as they will help ensure you do not stray from the main topic. The topic or theme is given to you in the opening line of the task. As listed under 'Common prompts and topics' some examples include: the environment, being healthy, digital devices, friends, and a place you have visited. You must keep all of your writing aligned to the topic/theme.

What do we mean by 'persuade/argue'? In some cases, it will be enough to state your opinion and then try to persuade your reader(s) to consider or even adopt your view. Sometimes, you will be asked to make a case – for example whether you agree with deforestation, the mass removal of trees – and here you can present an argument either for it or against it. In Task 4, you don't need to consider both sides of an issue – you only need to convey your opinion, backing this up with supporting detail.

The present tense is the most appropriate for Task 4 because you will be considering contemporary topics and themes. You can give examples of events in the past – and potential actions in the future – but your writing should be rooted in the present.

You are provided with plenty of space on the examination paper (usually two sides of A4) to write your response, so there should be no need to use extra paper. Aim for 150 words so you can give yourself the best opportunity to show your writing skills.

Examiner Input

In longer responses, structure and sequence are more important and an examiner will be looking for a pathway through the writing to be able to award higher marks. Less effective responses tend to be more random in approach, suggesting that planning and sequencing have not been done properly. Therefore, make sure that there is a logical way through your writing that a reader can follow. You should stay with your main idea and not drift away from it but should be adding supporting details to each main point.

In Task 4, you are given only two bullet points so it's a good idea to try to stay close to the ideas set out in these. The examiner will not be able to award you marks if your content loses relevance to the task. You must stay relevant to the topic and the scenario.

Exam Tip

In Task 4, the topics that occur in Theme one and Theme two are common ones, such as technology in everyday life, activities involving many people, healthy and unhealthy living, the environment, poverty, tourism – in other words, topics that can be debated from different points of view. These are usually topics that are of interest to all of us, no matter where we live in the world.

Assessment Objectives

W2, W3 and W4. Task 4 allows you much more control over the content and detail you choose, and how you organise and present it. In W3, you are assessed on all four parts: vocabulary, grammar, punctuation, and spelling. Note that the marking scheme has an extra achievement level at the top – Level 5 – for language skills, and also there are more marks available for language than content/communication. This is clearly an opportunity to demonstrate your range and skill of using language. W4 is how you can gain higher marks. The examiner will be looking at how well you have controlled your language and manipulated it (handled it with skill). As with Task 3, but more so, you will produce some creative and flowing (fluent) writing based around a topic that you can engage with.

Task 4

Now let's have a go at an example of Task 4 and the approach you should take.

Before you look at anything else in this section, write your response to the task that follows.

---

04 Write an article for your school or college website about activities that can be done in free time.

You could write about:

- **how much** choice there is for free-time activities for people your age

- **why** it's important to make sure we have enough time for such activities.

Your article should be between 100 and 150 words. **[23 marks]**

_____

_____

_____

_____

_____

_____

_____

_____

_____

_____

_____

_____

_____

_____

_____

_____

_____

Examiner feedback and raising my grade

Now that you have written your response to Task 4, look at the four sample responses below, and the guidance, tips, and advice offered.

Achievement levels

Here is a final reminder of the criteria that apply to all of the Writing paper tasks:

- **Content and communication:** You can think of this as how clearly you have conveyed the content you have chosen to write about to your reader.

- **Language:** This is your accurate, appropriate, and varied use of words, phrases, punctuation, sentences, and structures.

For Task 4, there are five levels available for content and communication (as there were for Task 3). However, for language, there are six levels, and the additional level at the top. This is to reward higher level use of language, and there are more marks available for Task 4 for language (15) than for content and communication (8).

Sample answers to Task 4

Sample response – Student 1

> I not have time for activety. However I do sometimes shoot hops with my friends, we make time for this on Saturday 5 pm. All togethor we have about 10 persons. We play two ends or 1st team to 50 points. Afterwards, we have free time also to go to eating food and drink in the next rode. Last time we lose 50–48. Great close.
>
> My age group must find thing to do around here. Colege is best for active. Outside we have basketball to shoot the hops. My idea is maybe more thing ages ago but not these day. It's not sure why, maybe not enough money.
>
> Staying fit is prime. Sad but many friends I have they too much unfitt.

Examiner Feedback

Achievement levels

Content and communication			
Level 4	Level 3	Level 2	Level 1
		✓	

This response from Student 1 is satisfactory and is generally relevant. However, sometimes her messaging breaks down.

- Student 1 has not fully understood the suggestion that we need to make sure we all have time for activities – instead she focuses on her own time and availability.

- She does respond to the amount of choice that people her age have locally, but she's not clear why this has changed over time.

- Student 1's final line shows understanding of the need for exercise through activities.

Language

Level 5	Level 4	Level 3	Level 2	Level 1
			✓	

Student 1's language shows some clear attempts at variety. Her writing conveys some clear meaning. She has more accuracy than inaccuracy.

- Her spelling is weaker with several errors.
- Her punctuation is good, except some missing punctuation to break up sentences.
- She tends to use simple sentences.

Examples of mistakes to avoid:

✗ 'I not have time' – 'not have' is often used where 'don't have' is the correct expression. However, to say, for example, 'I do not have any facilities for sport in your area', is correct English. Most of the time, you will use the contraction, such as 'I don't have any time for football' or perhaps 'I can't find the time'.

✗ 'about 10 persons' – In modern English, 'people' is the plural of 'person'. You should avoid using 'persons' in your writing, as it should only be used for special reasons (such as in legal cases). You can use 'peoples', but be sure you are talking about the plural of groups of people, such as 'the peoples of the South American rainforests'.

Sample response – Student 2

Free-time activities are not exactly part and parcel around here. We are lucky I guess to have a wide choice, from sports places from entertainment, to fun. It important. Because students aged teenagers have a lot of pressure and we need a way out from them. This is by having something to do with friends away from the study. It good. Because should keep a health mind and strong body.

On the hole, all of us here have a good choice so we take granted. Our town is small but safe. Inside it we have bowling ally, tennis club, cinema with 10 screens, skate park that I like with my group. I know one person from college who plays ches and she go to ches club. There seem to me a lot of choice around so I never really worry about it.

Examiner Feedback

Achievement levels

Content and communication			
Level 4	Level 3	Level 2	Level 1
	✓		

This is a good response from Student 2. It is almost always relevant, but there are one or two places that are unclear.

- 'Because students aged teenagers have a lot of pressure' isn't as clear as it could be, but we get the idea Student 2 is conveying in response to the 'why' part.
- 'Inside it …' and 'that I like with my group …' are two examples of unclear expressions, but these don't affect our understanding.

Language				
Level 5	Level 4	Level 3	Level 2	Level 1
		✓		

Student 2's language is generally accurate and his structures show the use of some complex sentences.

- He slips up with 'whole', 'alley', and 'chess'. Alley is a more difficult word to spell. Student 2 has used the homophone for whole (hole), and ches is close but not correct.
- His second paragraph has more complex sentences. He could have easily made two of his sentences in the first paragraph complex, but he chose to go for an effect by using 'Because'. It's not a good idea to start sentences with 'because'.
- His verb tenses are faulty and this is the main weakness of the response.

Examples of mistakes to avoid:

✗ 'part and parcel' – 'This is an idiom and it doesn't really work here. It has been used in English for more than 500 years. It means something that is a basic or an essential element. We can see from the context that Student 2 doesn't know how to use the idiom. This is a common error and we recommend you only use idioms if you are sure of their meaning, and their appropriate context.

✗ 'It important./It good.' – These are not correct grammar and not complete sentences because they need a verb. Remember to include a verb even in short expressions. 'It is good' (or shortened to 'It's good') and 'It is important' (or shortened to 'It's important') are fine. However, note that in both cases Student 2 could have written longer, complex sentences.

Sample response – Student 3

We make owner activty not in my area. Should be more over their but not sure why not. Culd be consil don't give no. Consil have money cos I see new and new for the under 5 in my area might be teens is not part of there plane.

Despite this you agerie with me I think from no time to leaving school it just homework Week end I do go running or player some with teem game but on parc not in spesial place as expenssif.

My opinnion is should be more yes it bad teens not get board and not caus trubble.

Examiner Feedback

Achievement levels

Content and communication			
Level 4	Level 3	Level 2	Level 1
			✓

This is a limited response, but it does have some relevance to the task. There are frequent places where Student 3 is unclear and the reader struggles to understand.

- 'We make own activty not in my area.' We can infer what Student 3 means here; that they have to find their own things to do to be active. However, we think he means because there isn't much to take part in, in his area – rather than making their own activities in a different place. He does say next that the council could be to blame.

- '… player some with teem game but on park not in spesial place as expenssif.' We also need to unpick this. What does Student 3 mean by a special place? Perhaps he means a sports ground that charges an entrance fee, unlike the park which is free.

- He fails to address the first bullet point – the 'why' part. Instead, he focuses on the lack of choice and does engage briefly with the context of people his age.

Language				
Level 5	Level 4	Level 3	Level 2	Level 1
				✓

Student 3's language has frequent errors and a narrow range of vocabulary and sentence structures.

- Student 3 spells these words incorrectly: could, council, plan, agree, team, special, expensive, bored, cause, trouble.

- Student 3 does not use any commas.

Examples of mistakes to avoid:

✗ 'over their/there plane' – As here, 'their' and 'there' are often confused with each other. Remember that 'their' is a determiner and you can think of it as 'belonging to', whilst 'there' is an adverb, usually used as an adverb of place or position. For example, 'The sports centre is over there'.

✗ 'bad teens not get board' – Student 3 has mistakenly used the homophone of 'bored'. Remember that a homophone is a word that is pronounced the same as another word, but the spelling and meaning are different (for example 'board' and 'bored'). (Remember that homonyms have the same spelling, but a different meaning, for example 'bored' – an adjective meaning having nothing much to do, and 'bored' – a verb meaning having made a hole by drilling or digging.)

Task 4

Sample response – Student 4

Have you left college and wondered what to do to take your mind off the next assessment. Me too. Well, here is my idea. Sports are not for everyone, so it's the responsibility of the local council to be sure that people our age have a good choice and that isn't just kicking a ball.

Teenagers need a release – in a safe and not threatening place – sports can do that, yes. Similarly, so can music and I would like to see more places where teenagers can be creative where we they explore other talents and get that pressure release they need.

To make time, design your own activity schedule because if you don't, you will find yourself distracted. It's too easy to reach for the smartphone or the ipad and that's a few hours gone by. Let's get together on this and form some different activity clubs; not like the predictable ones adults do for us. Are you with me?

Examiner Feedback

Achievement levels

Content and communication			
Level 4	Level 3	Level 2	Level 1
✓			

This is an excellent response, which is clear, fully relevant and detailed.

- It is 160 words long, so just outside the suggested range. However, the extra words are all relevant. In fact, they add to the flair
- Student 4 shows a strong sense of audience and an awareness that her readers are looking at a website article. She draws them in well and keeps their attention.
- The response takes the issue of a lack of range of activities and focuses on offering more creative activities.

Language				
Level 5	Level 4	Level 3	Level 2	Level 1
✓				

Student 4 uses sophisticated language techniques with some flair. She achieves an effect through her choice of expressions. This is confident and fluent writing.

- Only minor errors occur, such as missing the question mark after the rhetorical question.
- She probably needed a conjunction immediately after the second dash, as the sentence doesn't flow fully if the clause inside the dashes is removed. But this is a very minor error.
- She uses the semicolon with good effect.
- The discourse marker 'similarly' is well chosen.

Examples of mistakes to avoid:

✗ *Have you left college and wondered what to do to take your mind off the next assessment.* – Student 4's English is of a very high level. However, if you use a rhetorical question – which is a question that you don't expect your reader or audience to actually answer – you still need to use a question mark.

✗ *Teenagers need a release – in a safe and not threatening place – sports can do that, yes.* – Remember that if you use dashes to signpost additional information (in the same way as brackets), make sure that either side of the dash works as a complete sentence. In this case, Student 4 hasn't quite been fully effective. Can you see why? All she needed to do was add 'and' before 'sports'.

Language Support

1 In longer pieces of writing, it's useful to include **discourse markers** as signposts, so that your reader can navigate through your sentences and paragraphs. Try to make this as easy as possible by controlling the sequencing. Conjunctions and connectives are the means to do this. Student 2 tries to use a good discourse marker with 'On the whole', but unfortunately spells 'whole' as the homophone 'hole'. Student 1 has an effective discourse marker with 'Afterwards, we have free time …'. Student 3 uses 'Despite this …', which is a good discourse marker, but not effective in the context because Student 3 isn't in control of it. Can you see why not? Student 4 avoids the use of 'however' in preference for a much better marker: 'Similarly, so can music and I would like to see more places …'.

2 An effective **topic sentence** helps readers get the main idea of your paragraph quickly. It's a good idea therefore to think carefully about how you begin a new paragraph. For Task 4, you are writing between 100 and 150 words and this probably means three or four paragraphs. Remember, you are in control and the reader(s) will expect to be guided by you. We recommend you use a topic sentence for all of your paragraphs for Task 4. A good example of one is used by Student 4 in the third paragraph: 'To make time, design an activity schedule because if you don't, you will find yourself distracted.' From this we know what is coming – supporting detail about how you can be distracted and how you can take responsibility yourself. Topic sentences are most effective if they are short and punchy, and focus only on the main ideas in the paragraph.

3 **Modal verbs** can also help you to control your writing. Modal verbs, such as 'may/might', 'can/could', 'must', and 'will', can be used to show whether something is possible or certain, or to indicate obligation and ability. Student 1 writes that teenagers 'must find thing to do around here', and this is a good use of a modal. Student 2 writes 'Because should keep a health mind …', whilst Student 3 uses a modal to express possibility by writing 'might be teens is not part of there plane'. Despite some other errors here, Student 3 does use a modal with some skill because we are not sure in this case if the council has considered teenagers' needs locally. Student 4 uses the modal verb 'would' nicely in combination with the verb 'to like' to express politely what he wants in 'so can music and I would like to see more places …'. Did you also note that Student 4 uses a second modal verb in this short clause?

Exam Tip

Remember to leave some time at the end of the examination to check your writing. We gave you a suggested method for this in the Task 3 section, but as you will have written more than 100 words for Task 4, we suggest you read your work (in your head, so not to disturb others!), which may help you to identify words and phrasing that don't make sense or quite fit. This can also help you to spot missing punctuation or remove punctuation that is not needed. Your aim is to improve the rhythm of the writing and to carry out a light edit if needed.

In Task 4, the structure and sequence are very important so you can focus on these rather than a line-by-line search for mistakes. If you have time, do both. But if time is limited, the 'read in your head' check is the better approach.

4 Remember that words can usually be placed into three categories: positive, negative, or neutral. We refer to words that have a meaning (a feeling or an idea) that are beyond their actual or primary (main) meaning as **connotations**. To be able to manipulate your writing for Task 4, you need to understand a range of words that have these connotations. Think of a connotation as a hidden meaning of a word – a second meaning. For example, when Student 3 writes that it is expensive to take part in team games in the special place, what is really meant is that those places cost more money than Student 3 has or wants to spend. 'Expensive' is a word that can have neutral or negative connotations therefore. Student 2 uses the word 'pressure' to show stress. However, 'pressure' can also mean other things, such as the air in a vehicle's tyres, where it is neutral. Can you see how Student 2 uses it with a negative connotation? Could it have a positive connotation? Yes, for example in: 'I love the pressure of a game' or 'I need pressure to make me achieve my best.'

5 Remember to vary your use of language in Task 4, as this is how you will reach the higher levels and get more marks.

- Use a wide range of vocabulary and avoid repeating words. Try to use some words that have positive or negative connotations.

- Use short sentences for effect and show that you can control longer sentences by making them complex rather than simple or compound (coordinated).

- Write fluently by controlling signposting, so that a reader can follow your points and ideas smoothly. Use a range of different discourse markers and connectives.

- Be original and demonstrate your own language skill. Do not use pre-learnt phrases, idioms, or proverbs and 'make them fit'. An examiner will spot this immediately and it weakens your writing. An idiom must work in the context – you should not just drop an idiom in.

- Vary your use of punctuation in longer pieces of writing. Longer sentences need punctuating, so show that you are in control of this. Using one or two semicolons or colons correctly will improve your writing.

Model answer to Task 4

Making sure we have enough free time to take part in healthy activities is important for everybody. If we don't do this, several things could happen. We could become stressed by working or studying too much and our output will be lower. We could also get less fit or even ill, due to a lack of exercise.

Sharing our free time with friends or family also makes a bond that humans need. It's good sometimes to have friends outside of college, and to be always making new friends.

There is a lot of choice for younger people, especially teenagers. Where we live, we have a good range of sports facilities to use, but we also have community activities to help release us from daily life – such as music, drama, and travel-based clubs. However, as with many things in life, it's up to us to take advantage of what is there!

(147 words)

Revision Tip

Task 4 enables you to show your strengths. It's a chance to demonstrate sophisticated language, creativity, and flair. Here's the plan that Student 4 used to write her response.

- *Organise my writing into a logical sequence – analysing the task*

1	I need an article, for a website – this is the format and style I should use
2	My audience is readers from school/college – reach out to them at key moments
3	I'll start with the 'how much choice' part (not a lot for us <u>actually except</u> sports)
4	Main point will focus on 'why' – I'll focus on releasing pressure
5	But I'll also mention that we have a responsibility to make time for activities

- *Show progress clearly from beginning to end*

My opinion: there is not enough choice. I will offer an alternative to sports – making music. This helps with the creativity and the release teens need. I can finish with inviting people to respond by suggesting other alternative activity clubs.

- *Write a good introduction*

"Have you left college and wondered what to do to take your mind off the next assessment. Me too. Well, here is my idea. Sports are not for everyone."

That's a good opening – I will use a rhetorical question as it works well in the situation

- *Concluding paragraph – how can I end with a strong point/message?*

I have the topic sentence ready …

"To make time, design your own activity schedule because if you don't, you will find yourself distracted."

My concluding point is we shouldn't just rely on other people to provide activities for us.

Task 4

Here is a similar task. As revision practice, analyse it in the same way that Student 4 has done.

Write a blog entry for a sports magazine about doing sport for good health.

You could write about:

- **which** sports are good to get involved in
- **why** sport is good for your health

- *Organise my writing into a logical sequence – analysing the task*

  1

  2

  3

  4

  5

- *Show progress clearly from beginning to end*

- *Write a good introduction*

- *Concluding paragraph – how can I end with a strong point/message?*

How well did you do on Task 4?

Use the levels given to the four students, and look back at your response to the task to see where it fits best. This is your achievement level (examiners call this a band).

My levels for Task 4	Content and communication: Level _____ Language: Level _____
What I found difficult	
What I have learnt	
Five ways I can improve	• _____ • _____ • _____ • _____ • _____

If you would like a numerical score, use the grid below to decide on a mark depending on whether you feel your writing is stronger than the sample student answers, or perhaps not quite as good as theirs.

My mark for Task 4			
Content and communication	**My mark**	**Language**	**My mark**
N/A		Level 5 (13–15 marks)	
Level 4 (7 or 8 marks)		Level 4 (10–12 marks)	
Level 3 (5 or 6 marks)		Level 3 (7–9 marks)	
Level 2 (3 or 4 marks)		Level 2 (4–6 marks)	
Level 1 (1 or 2 marks)		Level 1 (1–3 marks)	
Total of the two marks for Task 4			_____ / 23

Reflecting on progress made and reaching higher levels

In this unit, you have had guided practice at completing a Writing paper with the aim of learning more about the skills you need to increase your performance in the examination. Now show all your written responses to your teacher for them to mark.

We have helped you strengthen your knowledge of what is required, we have recapped the key skills and Assessment Objectives, and you have applied these skills and your knowledge to help you feel confident and ready for the Writing paper.

On page 101 we asked you to estimate your levels of skills that are important to doing well in the exam. The table is repeated below. Don't look back at your original levels just yet – fill out the table below. Then compare the two tables and note what has changed.

Key skills	I think I need to improve in this area	I'm already quite good at this
Being clear about the purpose of my writing		
Keeping a strong focus on the audience – the reader(s) of my writing		
Choosing the correct style and register – do I have a wide range of types of writing?		
Being sure of the required setting and the broader context		
Using a wide range of vocabulary		
Using accurate spelling		
Using correct grammar, including my use of verb tenses to indicate past, present, and future		
Using accurate structures, connecting words and phrases, and a range of different sentence types		
The amount of relevant detail given in longer pieces of writing		

This is a reflective exercise and we want you to think about where you have improved.

• Do you feel that you have been able to recap all of the main skills needed for the Writing paper?

• Are you feeling confident about the range of themes and topics that you might be writing about?

• Do you have a good understanding now of how the Writing paper is constructed and how the tasks are set?

If the answer to those questions is positive, then you are well on the way to success.

Practice for the examinations

In this section you can complete a full set of practice exams. We suggest that you follow the times set on the front of the exam papers and that you complete the exams under exam-style conditions. You can do the exams at home. Find a quiet space where you will not be disturbed.

The answers are given at the end of the section. You will be able to mark your own Reading exam, and your Listening exam. You may need some help in marking your Writing. For Speaking, we offer you a photo card that you will not have seen before. We suggest you practise for this exam with an older member of your family, or perhaps an older, adult friend. We suggest that you record your Speaking test and ask your teacher to assess your performance.

Good luck!

Exam-style questions

Reading paper

Instructions

- You must answer the questions in the spaces provided. Do not write outside the box around each page or on blank pages.

Information

- The marks for questions are shown in brackets.

- The maximum mark for this paper is 60.

- You must **not** use a dictionary.

- If you need extra space for your answer(s), use a separate piece of paper.

Time allowed: One hour, 15 minutes

Text 1 Email

Read the first part of this email from Alex to Mia.

Answer questions **01** to **03**.

> Dear Mia
>
> 1   It was great to meet up yesterday with you and the group in Manchester. I caught the 5pm train to get home. There was a delay due to strong wind, so it was a four-hour journey and not three to London. The delay helped me to make my mind up.
>
> 2   I'm going to take a year off before I go to university in Leeds. I don't think I'm ready for full-time education yet. I think a gap year will give me a lot of benefits. Also, I will be more confident starting my degree course when I am 19 rather than 18.
>
> 3   What is the next step, Mia? You told us about an opportunity to spend six months in South America, working on a charity project with young female sportswomen. How do I get involved in that?

Write the correct letter in the boxes for questions **01** to **03**.

01 How many hours was Alex's train journey?

A	Three
B	Four
C	Five

[1 mark]

02 Where will Alex continue his studies?

A	Leeds
B	London
C	Manchester

[1 mark]

03 What is the **main** point of **paragraph 3**?

A	Alex is asking where the next meeting is.
B	Alex is asking what he should do to proceed.
C	Alex is asking for details about the specific location.

[1 mark]

Read the second part of the email.

Answer questions **04** to **06**.

4 I am really excited about helping young athletes. When I was 14 I joined my local athletics club in North London. I won all of the 800 metres races. I was also quite fast over the 200 metres distance but my best for the shorter distance was only a third place.

5 In South America, I would like to be the athletics trainer. I know that Aisha is also interested in sport but she said she doesn't like running. She said she prefers swimming. At our next group meeting in March, I'm happy to give a talk about my running skills. I run daily and I enjoy running with others.

Alex

Write the correct letters in the boxes for questions **04** to **06**.

04 Read the following statements.

Which statement is correct?

A	Alex managed a second place at the 200 metres.
B	Alex was beaten once at the 800 metres.
C	Alex's best race was the 800 metres.

[1 mark]

05 Which statement is true about Aisha?

A	She is not interested in sports.
B	She would rather do swimming.
C	She likes to run.

[1 mark]

06 What is the **main** purpose of the email?

A	To inform Mia about going to study a degree
B	To share the role of athletics trainer with Aisha
C	To ask Mia about coaching athletics

[1 mark]

Text 2 The Electric Light Movie House

Read the information in the first part of this announcement made by a cinema.

Answer questions **07** to **10**.

Not just a cinema

1　The Electric Light Movie House is one of the oldest cinemas in Europe. It's first movie in 1920 was in black and white and with no sound. Unfortunately it closed down in 1939 and remained closed for 25 years. In 1964, it re-opened and has been a success ever since. Located in a quiet suburban street in north Berlin, it is quite tricky to find. The easiest route by car is to use South Street. However, once you arrive you will be greeted by very friendly staff.

2　Nowadays, the cinema offers much more than just films. Some of the things on offer are:

- games evenings – where you can team-up with others and have fun
- genre clubs – where you can meet people interested in your favourite film type
- coffee mornings – the catch is that you have to share snacks you have cooked
- director nights – when you can meet and pose questions to well-known film directors.

3　We are proud to be an independent cinema and we rely on income from two sources. Our main income is from the people who come to watch our movies. We also receive some money from the German Council of Arts, as we promote local and national film-makers. They paid for a large studio room where our film-makers meet to share their ideas and hopefully inspire each other.

07　When did the cinema first start showing films?

Write the correct letter in the box.

A	1920
B	1939
C	1964

[1 mark]

08　What is the best road to use to get to the cinema?　[1 mark]

_____

_____

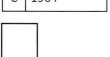

09 List **two** things the cinema provides that are **not** related to films. **[2 marks]**

1 _____

2 _____

10 Which of these statements best describes the **main** point of **paragraph 3**?

Write the correct letter in the box.

A	To describe the work of the German Council of Arts
B	To explain where the cinema gets its money from
C	To introduce local film-makers

[   ]

[1 mark]

Read the second part of the announcement.

Answer questions **11** to **14**.

4   Summer festival of film

Our latest project is an exciting one. We plan to run a film festival in July that will last two weeks. At the moment, we are open from Thursdays to Sundays. On those days, we have a full schedule, opening at 9 am and closing after our last film at 11 pm. During the festival we want to offer a broader range of things for people to take part in over the 14 days. We have never had such an event before and we are eager to make it a success.

5   How can you help us?

We are appealing to people who can help in a couple of ways. We will need extra hands to help show people to their seats for film viewings and serve them with drinks and snacks as they watch the films. We are also in need of events organisers. We have finalised our festival events, however, each event needs a person to rise to the task and carry the weight. We're looking for people who can take full responsibility to run an event.

6   Information for applicants

We want to meet you in person so don't contact us on social media! Please call in between 10 am and 3 pm and ask for our Festival Director, Sam Schenkel. She will be pleased to show you around and hopefully we can take things further. If so, we will arrange a formal interview after a few days. Don't worry if you have not had any experience working with movies or in a cinema. We seek enthusiasts more than experts!

11 Below is a list of statements about the information given in **paragraph 4**.

Two of the statements are correct.

Write the correct letters in the boxes.

A	The festival will take place before July.
B	The festival days will be Thursday to Sunday.
C	The festival will offer a wider range of activities.
D	This is the cinema's first ever festival.

☐ ☐

[2 marks]

12 In **paragraph 5** the writer uses the phrase 'rise to the task and carry the weight'.

Explain in your own words what this phrase means. **[2 marks]**

_____

_____

_____

_____

13 Below is a list of statements about the information given in **paragraph 6**.

Two of the statements are correct.

Write the correct letters in the boxes.

A	Applicants can go to the cinema to enquire about employment.
B	Social media can be used by applicants to show their interest.
C	Applicants will be offered an interview on the day.
D	Applicants do not need any knowledge of the film industry.

☐ ☐

[2 marks]

14 What is the **main** purpose of the text?

Write the correct letter in the box.

A	To promote its winter festival of film
B	To employ some assistants for a busy period
C	To offer a detailed account of its history

[ ]

[1 mark]

Text 3 What should we do with our junk?

Read the first part of this article.

Answer questions **15** to **19**.

1 A few weeks ago, I read in my weekly Science & Technology blog at school that part of an old space rocket weighing three tons crashed into the moon five years ago. Despite its weight, the impact on the moon was described as minor. However, it made me think about the whole idea of junk. What I mean by that is the wide range of things that we manufacture, sell, and use, but then at some point later decide that we don't need anymore.

2 The blog mentioned that there is a large amount of space junk that we no longer need floating around the Earth. Don't worry, these objects pose very little threat to us on Earth so our homes are as safe as houses. This is because a lot of space junk just burns up and disappears before it gets to us. There is a risk though of some space debris crashing into satellites which provide important services that are needed by mobile phone users.

3 The idea of an army of space junk above us is an environmental issue that in my opinion needs further research. I had never thought of junk causing us problems and even being dangerous. My image of junk was of a single item, sitting alone quietly and happily like a cat sleeping on a chair? It's a different image and more concerning when I think of a junkyard containing thousands of items all stacked up on top of each other, growing taller and taller.

15 Below is a list of statements about the information given in **paragraph 1**.

Which statement is correct?

Write the correct letter in the box.

A	Part of an old rocket hit the Earth five years ago.
B	Where the old rocket crashed it caused a major impact.
C	The moon suffered minor damage from an old rocket.

[1 mark]

16 In **paragraph 2** the writer says 'as safe as houses'.

Explain in your own words what this phrase means. [1 mark]

_____

_____

17 From **paragraph 2**, list three details about space junk. [3 marks]

1 _____

2 _____

3 _____

18 In **paragraph 3** the writer says 'an army of space junk above us'.

Explain in your own words what this phrase means. [2 marks]

_____

_____

_____

_____

19 What is the **main** point of **paragraph 3**?

Write the correct letter in the box.

A	A piece of junk is harmless.
B	Junk is harmless to the environment.
C	The increasing amount of junk is worrying.

[1 mark]

Read the second part of the article.

Answer questions **20** to **24**.

4   I have been researching this topic. During my research I interviewed several people. Here is what one of my teachers said: "Too many people are keen to have new items that they really don't need, discarding old items that end up as rubbish." My grandfather said: "Every time you go to a waste disposal centre these days, you will see many things that can be re-used. Like old bicycles, and pots and pans used for cooking." A shop owner told me: "It's different of course when old items have financial value. If they do, then people call them antiques, and trading them in can raise a lot of money at auctions."

5   My feeling is that people will only buy junk if it costs next to nothing. I suppose that's one of the reasons it ends up being thrown away. I think what people don't realise is that if we all keep throwing things away, junk just piles up.

6   We all must have the next generation phone, a shiny multifunctional laptop, the sleekest electronic bicycle, the top-rated video game. Perhaps people should change their mindset about their old items. For one thing, it is much better for the environment to re-use. We should try harder to share things we no longer want with other people around the world who might appreciate them. I've made my family take the plunge and sign on the dotted line with a website that offers this sharing service. I've also asked them to promise not to throw anything away.

20   In **paragraph 4** the people interviewed give their views on junk.

Which **four** things do they mention?

Write the correct letters in the boxes.

A	An unacceptable number of people must have new things.
B	When people buy new things they tend to re-use the old ones.
C	Old items usually end up as waste.
D	Waste disposal places contain nothing of any use.
E	Waste disposal centres contain a few items that can be re-used.
F	Items that are valuable are not called junk.
G	Selling items at auctions often results in a low income.
H	Buying and selling antiques is a healthy business.

☐ ☐ ☐ ☐

[4 marks]

21 In **paragraph 5** the writer says 'next to nothing'.

Explain in your own words what this phrase means. **[1 mark]**

_____

_____

22 In **paragraph 6** the writer says 'Perhaps people should change their mindset about their old items'.

What does this mean? **[2 marks]**

_____

_____

_____

_____

23 In **paragraph 6**, the writer says he has made his family 'take the plunge and sign on the dotted line'.

Explain in your own words what this phrase means. **[2 marks]**

_____

_____

_____

_____

24 Which statement best describes this article?

Write the correct letter in the box.

A	It solves the problem of junk in space.
B	It reports attitudes towards junk.
C	It argues that we all must have the latest items.

[   ]

[1 mark]

Text 4

In the following article, Miki, a climber, writes about her third major climb after years of training to become a professional climber.

Read the first part of the article.

Answer questions **25** and **26**.

1   I knew from a very young age that I would be a professional climber. When I was only seven years old, my father used to hang me from trees – he would tell me to go higher but also teach me how to get back down. He was a muscle-bound man and I trusted him entirely. He always reminded me it was safe, and he'd place what he called *Miki's Marshmallow* on the ground should I fall. It was actually a blow-up camping bed. When airless, it looked like a small block of square blue stone. But with my dad's giant foot overhanging the pump it took no time to take on its new life as my safety net.

2   My father had no training and at 15 years old climbed his first mountain. I have photographs of him when he was in his early 20s and he was born to do nothing but climb. He was of medium height, but sturdy and always sunburnt. The only ounce of unnecessary weight he had was in his long, blond locks.

---

25 In **paragraph 1** the writer says 'But with my dad's giant foot overhanging the pump'.

Explain in your own words what this phrase means.   **[2 marks]**

_____

_____

_____

_____

26 In **paragraphs 1** and **2** what does the writer say about her father's appearance?

List four things.   **[4 marks]**

1   _____

2   _____

3   _____

4   _____

Read the second part of the article.

Answer questions **27** to **31**.

3   My climbing apprenticeship was very different. From the age of 11 to 17 I was climbing regularly in a warehouse converted with specially designed climbing walls. The building had been used to hold grain so it had very high walls and a large open space. On a busy day, it was like a scene from a spy film, with people on ropes swinging from everywhere and nowhere. If you shut your eyes, the coldness helped you believe that you were scaling high peaks. The vastness of it made me feel like a wild sheep, able to roam freely.

4   Move the clock forward and I'm now 21. I'm stuck here on a ledge, 21,000 feet up, facing one of the highest peaks in South America. I'm on my third major expedition since those dreamy days of my apprenticeship. Back then, I never imagined I'd be spending a boring 24 hours with a laptop waiting for the mist to clear. The rolling mist feels quite warm. It's as if I'm in a creamy, soft blanket. I don't even feel damp as I have a waterproof coat on.

5   We're hardly the first to be here. On our way up, we stayed at several camps where the team was able to rest and check the equipment. I knew we were following a well-trodden path but was still surprised to see such vivid reminders of others. Scorched ground where tents had been pitched, the empty plots bitten down to the rock by hungry goats. I noticed shiny granite outcrops where tools had been sharpened. I found a dusty old climber's axe which I think had been left to be of some use. It's not exactly pristine up here.

27 In **paragraph 3** the writer says, 'The vastness of it made me feel like a wild sheep, able to roam freely'.

Explain in your own words what this phrase means.   **[3 marks]**

_____

_____

_____

_____

_____

_____

28 In **paragraph 4** the writer says, 'It's as if I'm in a creamy, soft blanket'.

What does this phrase mean?

Write the correct letter in the box.

A	She feels cold.
B	She feels re-assured.
C	She feels threatened.

[ ]

                                                                        [1 mark]

29 What is the **main** point of **paragraph 4**?

Write the correct letter in the box.

A	To convey the reality of climbing
B	To write a story on her laptop about climbing
C	To check her clothing because of the conditions

[ ]

[1 mark]

30 In **paragraph 5** the writer mentions evidence that other climbers have made the journey that she is making.

List **three** pieces of evidence she gives. **[3 marks]**

1 _____

2 _____

3 _____

31 Read **paragraphs 3** and **5** and choose **two** correct statements. Write the correct letters in the boxes.

A	Mika practised her climbing in an old grain store.
B	Mika's climbing centre is shared with a film crew.
C	Mika's team needed only one base camp to check equipment.
D	Mika's team used an established route.

[ ] [ ]

[2 marks]

Read the third part of the article.

Answer questions **32** to **35**.

6   Reliable communications are essential to get us to the top. The team have just radioed up and in 15 minutes the mist will clear. Conditions can change rapidly at altitude so we have to react in the blink of an eye. Optimum timing and grabbing your opportunities are crucial for achieving a mission's goals.

7   Fast-thinking doesn't usually help a professional climber's safety. Mistakes can be made with too much haste. It's better that we focus on the moment, often staying quite still to ensure the next step is the right one.

8   My father is part of my team. He doesn't climb but it's useful to have such experience in a team. He's not so brash these days. As he's got older, his safety checks take longer. It's a risky business climbing, and I am boldly taking on the family business.

32 In **paragraph 6** the writer says: 'we have to react in the blink of an eye'.

What does this phrase mean?

Write the correct letter in the box.

A	The team must prepare to move soon.
B	The team must be prepared to react immediately.
C	The team has about 30 minutes to prepare.

[1 mark]

33 From **paragraph 7**, list **two** things the writer suggests are sensible actions for professional climbers to stay safe. **[2 marks]**

1 _____

2 _____

34 From **paragraphs 6** to **8**, list four things that help to ensure the success of Miki's mission. **[4 marks]**

1 _____

2 _____

3 _____

4 _____

35 Which statement best describes the whole article?

Write the correct letter in the box.

A	It's an account of Miki's father's career in his younger days.
B	It's the story of a climber and her difficult and disappointing moments.
C	It's a reflection on Miki's younger years and where she is now.

[1 mark]

Exam-style questions

Listening paper

Instructions

- You must answer the questions in the space provided. You have 5 minutes to read through the question before the test starts.

Information

- The marks for the questions are shown in brackets.

- The maximum mark for this paper is 40.

- You must **not** use a dictionary.

Time allowed: 45 minutes

Task 1

Listen carefully to **Practice Paper Task 1** on the website. You will hear each statement twice.

Write the correct letter in the box for questions **01** to **04**.

01.1 How does the speaker want to travel to Italy?

A	By air
B	By rail
C	By road

[1 mark]

01.2 What does she say about the train journey?

A	There is plenty to see.
B	It is less relaxing.
C	It takes too long.

[1 mark]

02.1 How many items are needed when applying online for the visa?

A	One
B	Two
C	Three

[1 mark]

02.2 What is needed for the online process?

A	Attending an interview
B	Writing an email
C	Uploading a photograph

[1 mark]

03.1 When do the tickets need to be collected?

A	At 2.45pm tomorrow
B	By 10am today
C	Before 10am tomorrow

[1 mark]

03.2 What happens when someone is late?

A	They can enter anytime with a ticket.
B	They must wait until 3pm.
C	They are allowed in during the break.

[1 mark]

04.1 Why has the original trip been cancelled?

A	The bridge has been damaged.
B	The bridge is closed for a week.
C	The bridge has been destroyed.

[1 mark]

04.2 Why has the castle been chosen for the trip?

A	It has been hired for the day.
B	It is on high ground.
C	It has only minor damage.

[1 mark]

Task 2

Michael is speaking to his friend, Amina, about sharing an apartment in their second year at university.

You will hear each statement twice.

🎧 Listen carefully to the discussion in **Practice Paper Task 2** on the website and answer the following questions.

05 Give **two** things that Michael says are the benefits of **not** living in student accommodation? **[2 marks]**

_____

_____

_____

_____

06 List **two** tasks Amina mentions that are new to the students. **[2 marks]**

1 _____

2 _____

07 Give **two** examples of how the students' living costs have increased? **[2 marks]**

1 _____

2 _____

08 Give **two** ways that the students discuss that will help them exercise more. **[2 marks]**

1 _____

2 _____

Task 3

Anika, a teacher, is talking about how writing is an important part of her life.

You will hear each statement twice.

🎧 Listen carefully to the speech in **Practice Paper Task 3** on the website and fill in the gaps in the notes below.

09 Anika's diaries

Anika describes _____ her early diaries as a pleasure. **[1 mark]**

10 Her laptop

She can use the _____ of her laptop to make notes. It is light, so it is easy for her to

_____ in her bag. **[2 marks]**

11 The competition

The task was to cover someone's _____ life. I wrote about a family who

lived on a boat in the _____ The family had a problem one day with

_____ and they needed an expert to help out. **[3 marks]**

12 Anika's success

She did well in the competition and is _____ to have come second. The reward was a

camera which she uses for her _____. **[2 marks]**

Task 4

Simon is speaking to his trainer, Svetlana, about a charity bicycle ride he will be doing across Pakistan.

You will hear each statement twice.

🎧 Listen carefully to their conversation in **Practice Paper Task 4** on the website and answer the questions that follow.

13 In which direction will Simon be cycling? **[1 mark]**

_____

_____

14 What does Simon say is his **biggest** worry? **[1 mark]**

_____

_____

15 Svetlana is prepared for the ride.

List **three** ways she will support Simon. **[3 marks]**

1 _____

2 _____

3 _____

16.1 List **two** things that Simon asks his trainer to arrange at the end of the ride? **[2 marks]**

1 _____

2 _____

16.2 What message does Simon want to get across when he speaks at the end? **[1 mark]**

_____

_____

Task 5

Ryan is giving a talk about his new project which is sponsoring young piano players in his local town.

You will hear each statement twice.

🎧 Listen carefully to his talk in **Practice Paper Task 5** on the website and then answer the questions that follow.

17 What did Ryan **not** enjoy when he was a musician? Write the correct letter in the box.

A	Playing on stage
B	Travelling to the concerts
C	Arriving at the venues

[1 mark]

18 Ryan states that he wants to 'give something back to the town that treated us so finely'.

Explain in your own words what this phrase means.   [2 marks]

_____

_____

19 Ryan discusses the opportunities that young local musicians will have.

List **two** that he mentions.   [2 marks]

1 _____

2 _____

20 Which of these guests will help to select the first group of students?

Write the correct letter in the box.

A	Local council members
B	Professional pianists
C	Teachers of music

[1 mark]

21 What are **two** messages that Ryan finishes his talk with?

Write the correct letters in the boxes.

A	Avoid using a telephone to get in touch.
B	There will be social events held soon.
C	Those who want to know more should stay behind.
D	It's important to resolve early issues quickly.
E	The next meetings will focus on social media.
F	The next step will be to form specific groups.

☐ ☐

[2 marks]

Transcripts

Task 1

F1 If I could go away for a month I'd go to Italy. I could fly there but my choice is to go by train. I enjoy railway journeys. They might be slow but I feel relaxed and there are many sights to see along the way.

F2 For your visa, you start the application process online. You will need to upload a photograph and proof of address. Both are needed to prove your identity. Later, you will be interviewed in person. You will receive an email telling you the date and time of the interview.

F3 The show begins at 3pm and you will need to be in your seat by 2.45pm at the latest. Late arrivals will not be allowed in until the break after one hour. Your tickets must be collected at the box office at the theatre tomorrow before 10am.

M1 Please listen carefully. There is a change of plan and we will no longer be going to the bridge today. They have closed it for two weeks due to flooding that has caused minor damage. Our trip will now be to the castle which is on higher ground and dry.

Task 2

M1 Isn't it great to be living in an apartment in the city and not in the student halls at the university. There are no rules to follow, we don't have to be in our rooms by midnight and there's no signing-in book for guests.

F1 Along with freedom comes responsibility. There were things we just didn't have to do last year. I paid to use the Internet yesterday. Good that we are sharing that. We also need to register with a local doctor.

M1 I've just taken a part-time job as I'm aware that our expenses have gone up now that we're independent. There are train tickets to purchase four days a week, and we have to pay for our own energy bills. Oh, and I'm spending much more on food.

F1 On the bright side, I feel more healthy. I'm able to eat a lot more salads and fish. But you're right, healthier food is not cheap.

M1 I use public transport too often. I think I'm lazy. I'll try walking to the train station instead of catching a bus. That would be good for me. My bag is heavy so that will help build up my upper body strength.

F1 I think we can both do more exercise. I know it's a bit risky at times on the roads but using our bikes to get to university will make us fitter. They're just getting dusty at the moment.

Task 3

F1 When I was younger I always kept a diary. It was like a best friend. It was a handwritten diary, and I made sure that I wrote something in it every single day. I was ten years old when I wrote my first entry and I kept up my diary for seven years. I still have the books, and now and again I find it a real pleasure when I'm reading them.

F1 I'm now a teacher of English at a language school in Amsterdam. I still enjoy writing by hand but most of my work is word-processed, so my best friend is now my laptop. What I like about it is that I can handwrite onto its screen, and it converts my writing into text. It's great for making notes during lessons. The laptop is also quite light so I don't notice the extra weight when I carry my bag.

F1 I entered a diary writing competition a few months ago. The task was to write about daily life, and we could make up the characters involved. I chose a family who spend their summers on a boat. I wrote about one day when their boat was taken over by about 20 frogs! A Dutch specialist on amphibians was needed to ensure the frogs were not harmed.

F1 I came second in the competition and the story I wrote about the family was published – which makes me very proud. I also received a prize. It was a state of the art video camera. At the moment I'm collecting information on the workers who built the canals in Amsterdam. I'm speaking to local people to get some background details, and the camera helps me record my research.

Task 4

F1 The dates are confirmed now, Simon. We will spend five days in Lahore getting used to the climate and local conditions. We expect the temperature to be about 33 degrees Celsius and we should have a lot of dry weather and sunshine. Your route will take you south-west, all the way down to Karachi. Our flight leaves Birmingham airport on the 16th February. Oh, and no need to pack any winter clothes.

M1 You make it sound like an easy ride, Svetlana, by saying 'all the way down'. Didn't you say that there are some major hill climbs? One of them, a 4500 metre climb. That's going to be hard work, even for me and it's going to be more of a challenge in those high temperatures. What about the condition of the road on those mountain routes? I've heard there are some large holes. They are what concern me most. They might cause damage to the bike as it's not designed for rough roads.

F1 We will check the road ahead each morning to make sure it's not blocked. We will also patch up any holes. We have cement loaded onto the support vehicle. The vehicle is ready to go. The charity have been very generous in providing supplies, Simon. They have also arranged a big event on the finishing line. It's right by the sea, so I'm sure you'll enjoy the cool sea breeze. About the heat, we've loaded twice the amount of energy drinks we'd usually take to deal with the dehydration, and we've also ordered high factor sun block lotion.

M1 Yes, I'm looking forward to that. The organisers are interviewing me soon after I cross the line, so can you please make sure I can have 10 minutes cool down time. I'll need to collect my thoughts. Also, I'd like to offer a gift to them, so can you sort that out please. Ideally, something in our team colours. Can you also make sure the bike is stored away safely. It's great to support the charity but also it's important to let the people gathering know that I'm representing our UK-based professional team.

Task 5

Good afternoon and welcome to today's session. If I may, I'd like to start by telling you about my own life and career in music. For a very long time, I was the keyboard and piano player in a successful band. We were well-known and we recorded lots of studio albums. We played concerts all over the world. I enjoyed performing at different places but I often got bored with the long road trips to the venues. My best memories are concerts we played in Japan. I enjoyed Japanese culture and I actually lived there for a few years.

Fast forward to today and here we are in the Town Hall. Thirty years ago we played here in front of about 2500 people. You can imagine how I feel now on the same stage. It's bringing back a lot of good memories. Our violin player did a solo performance that night for about 20 minutes. I'm now living in my hometown, where I went to school, and I want to give something back to the town that treated us so finely.

I'm working with the town council on an exciting new venture. We are targeting students aged 15–18 at local schools who are keen pianists but don't have access to equipment to practise. Inside the hall, we have allocated two rooms. One room will be our instruction room, where the young people can develop their playing skills. Opposite is our second room, and it's a full digital recording studio, so they have a great chance to record their work. I'm excited by this as I plan to spend a lot of time messing about in there!

Some of you in the audience work for the council and some of you teach music in our schools. We feel that the latter group is in the best position to help us find suitable candidates. I will help as the Musical Director, and my colleague sitting on the front row is our Programme Director. We both feel that we are on the crest of a wave as we seek out new local talent. For the professional musicians in the audience – sorry, but we'd rather you aren't involved in the selection process.

Please get in touch soon with any questions you have. You can use the telephone line of course, but we have also set up a social media group to use. Let's allow a couple of weeks to get queries sorted swiftly, and then we propose meeting in small focus groups. It'll be more efficient to branch off into our specific skills areas. I did think about playing us out with a piano solo but it's getting late and we can't afford to wait.

Exam-style questions

Speaking test

> ### Candidate's material – Photo card
>
> To be conducted by the teacher-examiner.
>
> Time allowed: 10 minutes (+ supervised preparation time of 10 minutes)
>
> The test will consist of two parts:
>
> **Part 1**   **Photo card (15 marks)**
>   Approximately 3–4 minutes
>
> **Part 2**   **General conversation (25 marks)**
>   Approximately 6–7 minutes
>
> ### Instructions
>
> - During the preparation time you are required to prepare the Photo card given to you.
> - You may make notes during the preparation time for use during the test. **You must not write on this card.**
> - Hand your notes and card to the teacher-examiner before the General conversation.
>
> ### Information
>
> - The test will last a maximum of 10 minutes and will consist of a Photo card followed by a General conversation. The Photo card is based on Theme one and the General conversation is based on Themes two and three.
> - You must **not** use a dictionary at any time during this test. This includes the preparation time.

CARD A Candidate's Photo card

- Look at the photo during the preparation period.

- Make any notes you wish to on a separate piece of paper.

- Your teacher will then ask you questions about the photo and topics related to **Technology in everyday life**.

Your teacher will ask you the following three questions.

- What can you see in the photo?

- How do you use social media?

- What are some ways that we use technology?

[15 marks]

Part 2   General conversation

For approximately 6–7 minutes you will take part in a conversation based on the themes not used in Part 1, spending about 50% of the time on each of the themes. As the Photo card in this paper is from Theme one, your conversation will focus on Themes two and three.

We suggest you find a partner or a parent to conduct the Speaking test as it is done in the examination and record the whole test. Remember that the Speaking test is a conversation so encourage your partner to use the questions as the basis for a two-way discussion.

You can then ask your teacher to listen to the recorded test and give you feedback on your performance.

In Theme two, your partner should ask you these questions:

Theme two – Local, national, international and global areas of interest

- What is there for young people to do in the area where you live?

- How have you helped a neighbour in the past?

- Which charity do you think most deserves support? Why?

- What are the best ways to keep fit and healthy?

- Why is it important that people eat healthily?

- What are the main problems faced by homeless people?

- What are the effects of global warming?

- Why do you think so many people like to visit other countries?

- Where have you been on holiday?

- What is your ideal holiday? Why?

And after about 3 minutes your partner should move to Theme three and ask you these questions:

Theme three – Current and future study and employment

- Which subject do you most enjoy studying? Why?

- Tell me about something that you have enjoyed at school.

- Explain why it is important to learn other languages.

- What could be done to improve your life in school/college?

- In your opinion, what makes a good teacher?

- What do you plan to study next year?

- What could be the advantages of going to university?

- Would you like to work in England? Why/why not?

- Why is it important to have a good job?

- Describe your ideal job.

[25 marks]

Exam-style questions

Writing paper

Instructions

- You must answer the questions in the spaces provided. Do not write outside the boxes around each page.

- If you need extra space for your answer(s), use the extra space provided on pages 181–182. Write the question number against your answer(s).

- Cross through any work you do not want to be marked.

Information

- The marks for questions are shown in brackets.

- The maximum mark for this paper is 60.

- You must **not** use a dictionary.

Time allowed: 1 hour 15 minutes

01 Look closely at this photograph from a travel guide.

Describe what you see in the photograph.

Your description should be between 30 and 50 words. **[9 marks]**

_____

_____

_____

_____

_____

_____

02 You are going to a festival.

Write a letter to a friend inviting them to go with you.

You **must** write about:

- **where** the festival will take place
- **what** type of festival it is
- **why** your friend should join you.

Your letter should be between 50 and 70 words. Do **not** write an address. **[12 marks]**

03 Write about a part-time job you are doing.

You **must** write about:

- **what** the job is
- **where** the job is
- the **main** tasks of the job
- **why** you like this job.

Your article should be between 70 and 90 words.

[16 marks]

04 Write an article for your school or college website about how young people benefit from using technology.

You could write about:

- **why** we need up-to-date technology
- **how** young people's lives have been improved by technology.

You should write between 100 and 150 words.   **[23 marks]**

_____

_____

_____

_____

_____

_____

_____

_____

_____

_____

_____

_____

_____

_____

_____

_____

_____

_____

Additional page

Write the question number against your answer.

Additional page, if required

Write the question number against your answer.

Reading paper

01	B
02	A
03	B
04	C
05	B
06	C
07	A
08	South Street
09	games evenings
	coffee mornings
10	B
11	C and D
12	rise to the task – to meet the challenge/try hard to complete a task
	carry the weight – to accept the workload/be responsible for the workload
13	A and D
14	B
15	C
16	Very secure/Well-protected/Sheltered/Not a risk/Not in danger
17	Any three of:
	Large amount of space junk
	Space junk is floating around the Earth
	Space junk is not much of a threat to us
	Space junk burns up and disappears
	Space junk can crash into satellites
	Space junk can cause problems for mobile phone users
18	'an army' = a large amount/a large threat
	'of space junk up above us' = collecting together around Earth/amassing around Earth
19	C
20	A, C, F, and H
21	Close to zero/a very low value/a very low amount

22   For 1 mark = people need to think again/people need to reflect/people need to adjust their attitude

For 1 mark = be positive about re-using /consider old as useful to others/think about how old items can be shared, not discarded

23   For 1 mark = commit to the action/get over being nervous and do it

For 1 mark = show agreement/show consent

24   B

25   For 1 mark = (her father's) large foot/(her father's) huge foot

For 1 mark = extending over the pump/bigger than the pump

26   Any four of:

Muscle-bound/muscular/lots of muscles

Medium height

Large feet

Sturdy

Sunburnt

Long/blond haired

Not overweight/an ideal weight/no unnecessary weight

27   For 1 mark = the huge size of the space

For 1 mark = she felt like a wild animal/she felt she was in a wild space

For 1 mark = she felt she could go anywhere and everywhere she wanted

28   B

29   A

30   Evidence:

Scorched ground where tents had been pitched

Outcrops of stone that were used to sharpen tools

A climber's axe

31   A and D

32   B

33   Focus on the moment

Stay still

34   Reliable communication

Optimum timing

Taking opportunities

Experience in the team

35   C

Listening paper

01.1 B

01.2 A

02.1 B

02.2 C

03.1 C

03.2 C

04.1 A

04.2 B

05 Any two of:

Not having to follow rules

No need to sign in guests (in a book)

No need to be in by midnight

06 Pay for the Internet

Register with a (local) doctor

07 Any two of:

Train tickets (have to be bought)

Pay the energy bills

Spending (much) more on food

08 Any two of:

Walking to the train station

Cycling/biking (to university)

Heavy bag builds up upper body (strength)

09 reading

10 screen + carry

11 daily + summer + frogs

12 proud + research

13 South-west

14 Large holes/damage to his bike

15 Check the road ahead for blockages/check to make sure the road is clear

Patch up any holes/fill in any holes

Loaded twice the amount of energy drinks/made sure that twice the normal amount of energy drinks are provided

(Ordered) high factor sun (block) lotion

16.1 10 minutes cool down time/10 minutes so he can cool down/10 minutes time to collect his thoughts

A gift

Make sure the bike is stored safely

16.2 That he is representing his UK team

17 B

18 For 1 mark = he wants to thank the town by offering something

For 1 mark = because the town was very kind to him and his band/ they were treated excellently/so well

19 Any two of:

They will have access to equipment.

They will have access to places to practise.

They can develop their playing skills.

They can record their work.

20 C

21 D and F